T5-BQA-652

DAVID AND HIS GOD
RELIGIOUS IDEAS AS REFLECTED IN BIBLICAL HISTORIOGRAPHY AND LITERATURE

JERUSALEM BIBLICAL STUDIES

Jerusalem Biblical Studies vol. 5

Translated from the Hebrew Manuscript by Ruth Debel

Edited by Ora Lipschitz

The "Jerusalem Biblical Studies" aims at publishing a series of monographs on biblical literature and its formation, the religion of Israel and ancient Near Eastern history.

DAVID AND HIS GOD
RELIGIOUS IDEAS AS REFLECTED IN BIBLICAL HISTORIOGRAPHY AND LITERATURE

Shamai Gelander

Simor Ltd.
Jerusalem 1991

JERUSALEM BIBLICAL STUDIES

Vol. 1. A. Rofé, *"The Book of Balaam" (Numbers 22:2–24:25)*. [Hebrew]

Vol. 2. T. Rudin-O'brasky, *The Patriarchs in Hebron and Sodom (Genesis 18–19)*. [Hebrew]

Vol. 3. E. Tov, *The Text-Critical Use of the Septuagint in Biblical Research*.

Vol. 4. N. Na'aman, *Borders and Districts in Biblical Historiography: Seven Studies in Biblical Geographical Lists*.

Simor Ltd.
POBox 39039, Tel Aviv 61390
ISBN 965-242-007-7

Printed in Israel
at the Ben Zvi Press, Jerusalem

TABLE OF CONTENTS

Foreword

Introduction 9

The Man of God 15
The Historical Connection 20
A Wrathful God 25
David's Plan and the Divine Plan 28

Chapter One: **Bringing the Ark up to Jerusalem — 2 Sam. 6** 33
The Uzzah Episode 36
Was it David who Sinned? 42
The Relationship of the Episodes of Uzzah and Michal 46

Chapter Two: **The Census and Stopping the Pestilence: 2 Sam. 24** 55
Excursus: Compariosn with 1 Chr. 21 59

Chapter Three: **2 Sam. 6 and 24** 69

Chapter Four: **Does the Lord 'Dwell in a House' or does he 'Move about in Tent and Tabernacle'? — 2 Sam. 7** 75
Approaches to the Story 75
Text and Composition 80
Ideas and Meaning 89
Past and Future 92
Nathan's Prophecy and David's Prayer 101
2 Sam. 7:26 102
The Scheme of 2 Sam. 7 105

Chapter Five:	**The Structure and Intention of 2 Samuel 5**	111
	General Characterisitics	114
	Detailed Analysis	115
	The Common Denominator	132
Conclusion		137
Abbreviations	Bibliographical Abbreviations	141
	Other Abbreviations	181
Indexes	Index of Biblical Passages	185
	Index of Authors	191
Hebrew Section		195

FOREWORD

Initially my study of David concentrated on literary research, but in the last seven years as my teaching repeatedly brought me back to the Book of Samuel, my interest shifted. Many of the ideas in this book have crystalized in the process of classroom dialogue with far too many students to be mentioned here. I am grateful for the opportunity I had for studying for them, with them and by them.

I am deeply indebted to all those who participated in advancing this study. To Professor A. Rofé of the Hebrew University in Jerusalem, to A. Macintosh of Cambridge and to Ruth Fiedler, whose remarks and council were a source of wisdom and inspiration - innumerable thankings.

Lots of gratitude are due to Ruth Debel for her impeccable translation of my Hebrew manuscript, and to Ruth Connel Robertson who by relentless and meticulous revision, taught me a brilliant lesson about precision and clarity in exposition and style.

Way and above am I grateful to the Simor publishers, who so graciously adopted me along with my script, endowing me with home and harbour, under the warm and generous auspicies of Ora Lipschitz, who knew no limits in supervising and coaching me in the intricate ways of scientific research, while enacting, in congenial partnership, her creative faculties as mentor and editor.

The English version used throughout this book is the Revised Standard Version [RSV]. Wherever it seemed necessary to follow another translation, it is explicitly stated.

Jerusalem, 1990 S.G.

INTRODUCTION

The more one delves into the personality of king David as portrayed in the Books of Samuel and referred to in the Books of Kings, the more one finds oneself preoccupied with the question: what made David such an incomparable symbol of ideal kingship, and a measuring rod for righteous rule and leadership? The facts of establishing the united kingdom of Israel and a stable dynasty which lasted more than four hundred years must not be underestimated but from the political, religious or legalistic points of view, the enterprises of other kings, such as the reforms of Josiah, Hezekiah or even those of Jehoshaphat may be considered no less significant a contribution than David's to the realization of Israel's religious concepts.

The attempt to find an answer to this question, and to others arising from it, was the reason for my plunging into this study, disregarding my own advice to students to avoid writing papers on extensive subjects. After all, what more remains to be said about king David?

I am trying in this book to present David's enterprises as seen by the biblical historiographer. In other words, the basic question of this work is: what does the historiographer wish to ascribe to David? Studies of David and his enterprise have dealt mainly with ideological or with textual and literary aspects. My purpose is to reach through textual and literary analysis the ideology that lies behind the stories.

The Kingdom of David is associated with many traditions, ideologies and concepts of faith. The usual approach is to consider David's ascent to the throne as the beginning of a new era, not only from the political, but from the religious standpoint. This stage is usually designated as the origin of the ideology of the 'choice of Zion'.

It is customary to see the earliest seeds of messianic ideas in accounts connected with this stage (e.g., in the prophecy of Nathan in 2 Sam. 7). Such ideologies — the place of Jerusalem in biblical faith, the choice of Zion as against the choice implicit in the Exodus, the covenant of David and the eschatological ideas associated with the monarchy — are undoubtedly the outcome of a long process.[1]

To the best of my knowledge, no research has pointed systematically to any direct contribution by David to the firm establishment of a new religious concept. In this study I shall attempt to show that the primary purpose of the texts we shall analyze is their theological message. They are: the bringing up the Ark from Kiryat-jearim (2 Sam. 6); the story of the census and the stopping of the plague on Araunah's threshing-floor (2 Sam. 24), the story of the prophecy of Nathan and David's prayer (2 Sam. 7), as well as accounts of other enterprises undertaken by David (primarily 2 Sam. 5). I shall also endeavour to show that those messages serve to form a single comprehensive theological concept. This may well lead to the conclusion that the editor-author responsible for the final formulation of the accounts[2] does not regard David's enterprises as merely a change or turning point but a 'revolution' in the realm of faith and religion.[3]

1. See Alt, "Jerusalem" (1925); and in general concerning the changes resulting from the establishment of David's kingdom. Alt, "Statenbildung" (1930), and esp. Rost, "Sinaibund" (1947); *Israel* (1937), and Zimmerli, *Theologie* (1971), differentiate between the traditions of David's covenant and those of the Exodus.
2. For the meaning of the term 'editor-author', in this book see note 41.
3. I shall endeavour to demonstrate that this understanding of David's enterprise is also expressed in the present sequence of the accounts in 2 Sam. 1–8 (see esp. Chapter Three). For a survey see: Gunn, *Story* (1978).

In my opinion, the most important thing about this revolution is in the preception of God: David's desire to build a house for the Lord, who until then had moved about in a tent and tabernacle (2 Sam. 7:6) cannot be explained only as a practical measure. Nor is it only a gesture inspired by the king's religious fervour. I shall attempt to show that this is a symbolic act meant to be the culmination of a series of measures motivated by a single purpose. The Lord who moves about is the tribal God, with all this implies about the way people perceived him. To a great extent, the lack of a permanent abode is also connected with the absence of permanent explicable principles. A wandering God is apparently also one prone to incomprehensible outbursts of fierce, destructive wrath. His revelations of Himself are often involved with mysterious manifestations, and there is no knowing when or if he will respond to his petitioners. His envoys, men of God or prophets, act accordingly. On the other hand, a God with a permanent abode is one whose manners and customs are evident, and their moral basis can therefore be explained. He does not give vent to inexplicable outbursts of wrath. The way He reacts, functions and intervenes in what transpires is less likely to be perceived as arbitrary or mysterious. The very fact that He is ensconced in a permanent abode also means that his response to petitioners is consistent, or at least has the clear, known element of constancy implied by routine.

The theological perception of this revolution seems to me to offer an apt explanation of certain manifestations that until now have been interpreted pragmatically. Thus, for example, the special closeness between David and the Lord, as revealed in various scenes and episodes has often been noted. It has been pointed out in particular that the Lord's detailed responses to David's requests for guidance exceed all the usual advice elicited from an oracle.[4]

4. It seems that a question to God, like any oracular query, either receives a blurred answer, requiring interpretation by an authorized individual (such as a priest), or has to be formulated so that it can be answered by a simple 'yes' or 'no'. It is therefore apparent from the answers David obtained (2 Sam 2:1, or

David asks not only whether to ascend to one of the cities of Judah, but to which one (2 Sam. 2:1). God not only promises David that he will deliver the Philistines into his hands, but even instructs him as to how and when to act (2 Sam. 5:19–20, 23–24). This is usually explained in terms of political ideology, not theology.[5] A current view is that the author stressed the Lord's answers to David's questions in contradistinction to His attitude to Saul, who was not vouchsafed any answer at all (see particularly 1 Sam. 28:6 "the Lord did not answer him, either by dreams or by Urim, or by prophets").[6] Similarly, the special favour shown to David in times of difficulty has been noted.[7] The answer of the Lord as transmitted by Nathan after David's offence in the case of Bath-sheba and Uriah comes surprisingly quickly: "The Lord also has put away your sin; you shall not die" (2 Sam. 12:13). In this matter, too, the conventional explanation[8] derives from the author's desire to emphasize the difference between David and Saul. God puts away David's sin at once because he did not hesitate to admit "I have

5:19) that he received special treatment by YHWH. See Budde, *Samuelbücher* (1902) pp. 193 ff.; Hertzberg, *Samuelbücher* (1960), pp. 222–225; *Samuel* (1964), pp. 272–275; Soggin, *Königtum* (1967), pp. 63 ff.

5. Carlson, *David* (1964) appears to be an exception. He divides all the material about David according to theological criteria, such as periods of blessing and periods of curse.
6. This is apparent in the works of the Jewish Medieval commentators. See *Midrash Shoher Tov,* Ps. 27; *Pesikta Rabbati,* 88. Still there is a tendency to moderate the usually rigid attitude towards Saul. e.g., on the phrase "...tomorrow you and your sons shall be with me" (1 Sam. 28:19), the disciple of Rabbi Ami Bar Abba, in the name of Rabbi Shmuel Bar Nahmani: Saul's death is more acceptable than his life, for in his life it has not been said tomorrow you and your sons will be with me, but at his death it had been said you and your sons with me — with me — within my seclusion. See also *Yalkut Shimoni,* 140, *Midrash Shmuel,* Berakhot 12/2. See also: Hertzberg, *Samuelbücher* (1960), p. 224; *Samuel* (1964), pp. 273–274; Grønbaek, *Aufstieg* (1971), p. 251; Abramski, *Kingdom* (1977), pp. 115–125.
7. See McCarter, *II Samuel* (1984), pp. 89–90.
8. See especially *Sanhedrin* 20:2; *Yoma* 22:1–2. For a literary analysis of Nathan's oracles and response to David's words in 2 Sam. 12, see Fokkelman, *Narrative Art* (1981), pp. 83–88.

sinned against the Lord" (2 Sam. 12:13) while Saul does not admit his sin until he has tried to argue his case, and even then he makes an excuse: "because I feared the people and obeyed their voice" (when explaining his war with Amalek, his taking of spoils and sparing the life of Agag — 1 Sam. 15:24).[9] God's intervention on David's behalf in the rebellion of Absalom is also explained by most commentators, traditional as well as modern, as part of the fulfilment of the divine plan. In accordance with this plan the Lord influences the outcome of the struggle for the throne,[10] as He promised. Conceding to David's prayer, "O Lord, I pray thee, turn the counsel of Ahithophel into foolishness" (2 Sam. 15:31), is explained in the text itself: "For the Lord had ordained to defeat the good counsel of Ahithophel, so that the Lord might bring evil upon Absalom" (2 Sam. 17:14).[11]

It appears that the commentators are interested in theological aspects only when political issues are involved. Anyone analyzing the story of Absalom's revolt from the military-historical or literary standpoint, must become aware that this is the only time in the entire broader context, i.e., in 2 Sam. 9–20, that the Lord intervenes during the course of events.[12] To the best of my knowledge the lack of intervention by God is not regarded by commentators as a special theological phenomenon. It seems to me that the consis-

9. See Abrabanel (in the name of Rabbi Joseph Albo): "... it was thought that Saul sinned as King, while David sinned as a man but not as a king". Cf. *Sanhedrin* 20:2 in the name of Rabbi Jossi: "... when they entered the land, they obtained three commandments: to set a king over them, to cut off the seed of Amaleq and to build the chosen House, and I do not know which comes first [English translation by A. Mishcon (London 1935)].
10. Rost, *Thronnachfolge* (1926); *Succession* (1982). For more recent bibliography see Garsiel, *David* (1975), pp. 132–139.
11. Whybray, *Succession* (1968), pp. 62–65; 71–75; Mazar, "David and Solomon" (1979).
12. Adar, *Narrative* (1959), pp. 160–206; Auerbach, *Wüste* (1938), pp. 229–235; Rost, *Thronnachfolge* (1926); *Succession* (1982); Garsiel, *David* (1975), pp. 126–153 (esp. 150–153); Whybray, *Succession* (1968), pp. 19–47.

tent response to David's appeals and requests, and God's minimal direct intervention, are opposite sides of the same coin, and both should be viewed as part of a single theological concept. In accordance with this concept the Lord protects the king and ensures the success of the monarchic enterprises because the works performed by David are a step towards the accomplishment of the kingdom of God.[13] The king is aware of this and knows that his reign depends upon the will and protection of the Lord. This idea will be discussed at length in Chapter Five. What it means is the existence of a mutual guarantee from now on. The Lord's role is no longer expressed through sudden, arbitrary intervention as was the case previously. The main purpose of the Lord's capricious behaviour had been to demonstrate His power, to ensure that His uniqueness would be recognized and He would be held in awe. Henceforth, when God intervenes, it is primarily to prevent the disruption of a divine plan that is to be brought to fruition by the king. This new concept is the outcome of the enterprises the editor-author wishes to attribute to David. In this study I shall try to show how the editor-author does this.

The assumption of a divine plan for the succession to the throne rests mainly on God's promise through Nathan (2 Sam. 7). Nathan's prophecy, and the many interpretations of it, as well as its theological aspects, will be examined in Chapter Four. It is my intention to show that the religious concept behind the story of the succession to the throne is essentially different from other stories in Johsua — Kings,[14] to such a degree that it may be said to reflect a

13. The idea of the 'Kingdom of God' will be discussed below note 56. In this context, when speaking about steps taken towards the accomplishment of the kingdom of God, I refer to the concept of God as controlling history.

14. De Wette, *Beiträge* (1806) was the first to indicate that the redaction of Joshua-Kings was done by the Deuteronomistic writers. In this context it is not necessary to decide whether there was a single redactor for the Former Prophets, i.e., Joshua through Kings, or whether there were a few.

different 'religious climate' and different basic concepts.[15] The fact that 2 Samuel concentrates on events that are part of life in Judah, while about half of the Book of Kings concentrates on events that take place in the Northern kingdom, may perhaps be a partial explanation, but the matter calls for detailed analysis.[16]

The Man of God

To simplify matters, in this study, the term 'man of God' will also be applied to one whom the Bible does not explicitly name as such,[17] although he fulfils the same functions, such as נביא (pro-

On the time of composition of the book of Kings see Greenberg, "Religion" (1979), pp. 79–85: "The final editing occurred between the latest historical datum in the book — the release of King Jehoiachin from prison in the accession year of Evil-Merodach of Babylon (561 BCE) — and the Restoration, which is beyond its horizon (538 BCE). The hybrid religion ascribed to the Samaritans in 2 Kings 17:24–41 also indicates a period anterior to the building of the Second Temple, since at that time the Samaritans were irreproachably YHWH-fearing (otherwise their idolatry would have been cited in the Jews' rebuff of their participation in the building of the Temple)". Cf. Haran, "Composition" (1979), pp. 1–14, and note 41 below.

15. Otto, agreeing with Soederblom, distinguishes between the stern and grim YHWH the national God, and ELOHIM the familiar and patriarchal God. He believes that the roots of the idea of YHWH are to be looked for in early animist notions. Soederblom, *Gottesglauben* (1915), p. 297; Otto, *Heilige* (1927), pp. 70–71; *Holy* (1969), p. 74. I doubt whether these distinctions still hold. It seems to me that ELOHIM, though patriarchal, is nevertheless grim, and YHWH also posseses familiar qualities. Noth, *Pentateuch* (1948), pp. 20–28; *Pentateuchal Traditions* (1972), pp. 20–27; von Rad, *Theologie* (1958), vol. 1 pp. 332–344; *Theology* (1962), vol. 1 pp. 334–347; Liver, "Kings" (1962); Haran, "Composition" (1979).
16. For a more detailed analysis see Noth, *Studien* (1943); *D History* (1981); von Rad, *Theologie* (1958) vol. 1 pp. 332–344; *Theology* (1962), vol. 1 pp. 334–347; Liver, "Kings" (1962); Haran, "Composition" (1979); Rofé, *Stories* (1988), pp. 75–105. On the Deuteronomistic redaction of the historical books see also: Hoffman, *Exodus* (1983) pp. 149–155. Cf. note 42 below.
17. Uffenheimer, "Prophecy" (1968), pp. 691–693; *Ancient Prophecy*, (1973), pp. 2–5, 278–280.

phet)[18] (e.g., Gad 2 Sam. 24:11 cf. 1 Chr. 21:9), חזה (visionary) and ראה (seer).[19] It is particularly important to pay attention to 1 Kings 20, in which a role almost identical with that of prophet is referred to in one and the same narrative as 'a prophet' (vs. 13), as 'a man of God' (vs. 28), and 'a certain man of the sons of the prophets' (vs. 35).[20]

The stories about men of God, in the books of Samuel and Kings, contain characteristics which manifest themselves repeatedly, so that it seems possible to speak of a pattern.

a. The man of God is often associated with a request to cure illness. Sometimes he is asked to heal (e.g., the story of the illness of Abijah son of Jeroboam. Jeroboam sends his wife in disguise to the prophet Ahijah at Shiloh to find out what will happen to the sick child, 1 Kings 14:1–8). Sometimes, however, the illness is only included in a story as part of a characterization.

> The man of God and Jeroboam in 1 Kings 13:1–6: Jeroboam, whose hand withered when he ordered the capture of the man of God who had come from Judah; Elijah in 1 Kings 17:17–24; Elijah and Ahaziah (2 Kings 1); Elisha (2 Kings 2:19–22, see also 3:19–22; 4:38–41); Elisha

For the term איש האלהים as a factor in determining the relationship between the Elisha and Elijah narratives, see Rofé, *Stories* (1988), pp. 133–134.

18. The modification of איש האלהים into נביא, seems to be connected with the diminishing role of prophecy in late biblical historiography, as pointed out by Amit, "Prophecy" (1983).
19. In 1 Sam. 9:8–9 three of the titles [איש האלהים, רואה, נביא] refer to one and the same individual.
20. The designation איש האלהים is frequently used in the books of Samuel, Kings and Chronicles, whereas in Joshua and Judges it is applied only to Moses (Joshua 14:6), except for Judges 13:6,8 where Manoah's wife identifies the Angel of God as איש אלהים.

who cures Naaman's leprosy (2 Kings 5); Elisha and Ben-hadad (2 Kings 8:7–15); the man at Elisha's grave (2 Kings 13:20–21); Isaiah and Hezekiah (2 Kings 20:1–11); and from a certain standpoint, Saul at En-dor (1 Sam. 28, particularly vss. 20–23).[21]

b. The words of a man of God, particularly when meeting a king, contain a surprising element, which can be defined as enigmatic.[22] Generally, but not always, this element appears at the beginning of an encounter. The surprise may be in his behaviour, although it is also associated with speech. As the story unfolds, it emerges that the enigma conceals within it the key to the solution of the problem, or contains the main message of the story.[23]

Samuel to Saul: "... And for whom is all that is desirable in Israel? Is it not for you and for all your father's house?" (1 Sam. 9:20), although actually Samuel's whole attitude to Saul on this occasion is enigmatic and surprising. He invites Saul to go up the high place before him (**עלה לפני הבמה**) and to eat with him, he saves a special portion of meat for Saul, and gives him **אותות** (signs) after anointing him (1 Sam. 10:2–6). The scene at En-dor in 1 Sam. 28, and particularly the words of Samuel in vs. 19: "...and tomorrow you and your sons shall be with me"; Ahijah, who secretly appoints Jeroboam to kingship (1 Kings 11:29–39); the man of God, who refuses to go with Jeroboam (1 Kings 13 esp. vss. 8–9); Ahijah, who recognizes Jeroboam's wife as soon as he hears the sound of her footsteps,

21. Uffenheimer, *Ancient Prophecy* (1973), pp. 289–292; Rofé, *Stories* (1988), pp. 60–70. On healing legends as part of the struggle against the worship of Baal, see Bronner, *Elijah* (1968), pp. 86–122.

22. Uffenheimer, *Ancient Prophecy* (1973), pp. 281–284; Rofé, *Stories* (1988), pp. 58–60.

23. I am not concerned with the element of magic, but with the connection between the personal event and its political background. See also Rofé, *Stories* (1988), pp. 55–58.

although she pretends to be someone else (1 Kings 14:6); Elijah, who instructs the woman in Zarephath to make a cake for him (1 Kings 17:13); the prophet who promises Ahab that all the multitude of Aram shall be delivered into his hands (1 Kings 20:13–14); again, a man of God who promises the king of Israel to deliver the Arameans into his hands, because they have said that "The Lord is a god of the hills, but he is not a god of the valleys" (1 Kings 20:28); one of the 'sons of the prophets' who asks his neighbour to strike him (1 Kings 20:35–37); Micaiah, who changes his prophecy to the king (1 Kings 22:15 cf. vs. 17); Elisha, who forbids the king of Israel[24] to kill the Arameans who were brought into Samaria (2 Kings 6:22); Elisha, who instructs Hazael to tell the king of Damaskus that he would recover, although the Lord had shown him "that he shall certainly die" (2 Kings 8:10); the way Elisha instructs one of the sons of the prophets to anoint Jehu, and the way the latter fulfils the instructions (2 Kings 9:2–3, 6); Elisha, Joash and the arrows (2 Kings 13:18–19).

c. The actions of the man of God, especially when meeting a king, often verge on the miraculous, although in no sense is he represented as actually practicing magic.[25]

The signs Samuel gives Saul (1 Sam. 10:2–10); the man of God and the sign he gives Jeroboam (1 Kings 13:4, in addition to the symbolic act of tearing down the altar, vss. 3–5); Ahijah telling Jeroboam's wife in detail, very much like a sign: "When your feet enter the city, the child shall die" (1 Kings 14:12); Elijah and the captains of the fifty (2 Kings 1:9–11); Elisha and Jehoram and the minstrel (2 Kings 3:14–20); Elisha and Naaman (2 Kings 5:10, 14); Elisha and Gehazi (2 Kings 5:27); and apparently also the story of

24. On the question of the identity of the king in 2 Kings 6:22, see Gray, *Kings* (1964), pp. 430 ff.; Rofé, *Stories* (1988), pp. 70–74.
25. Uffenheimer, *Ancient Prophecy* (1973), pp. 278–284.

Elisha warning the king of Israel against Aram , as it is not clear how Elisha knew the site of the Aramean camp (2 Kings 6:9–10).

Very close to these are the symbolic acts interpreted by the man of God performing them, such as tearing the garment by Ahijah the Shilonite (1 Kings 11:29–39).[26] Certain incidents are almost magic and might well be defined as borderline cases, such as the story of the bow and arrows told about Elisha and Joash (2 Kings 13:14–19).[27]

I shall not go into the details of other cases in which quasi magical elements are prominent,[28] but a few general remarks about the acts performed by Elisha may be helpful. He is portrayed as functioning independently, addressing no prayer to God, not even mentioning Him, whereas when similar deeds are recounted of Elijah, his reliance on God is a central factor.[29]

I have cited above stories about kings and men of God and their relations, i.e., historical figures, events and situations. This I believe, removes them from the realm of tales, or legends, about individuals, and makes them part of history, primarily in that they

26. Uffenheimer, *Ancient Prophecy* (1973), pp. 168–169 points out the negative attitude towards Solomon and his reign in the speech of Ahijah (1 Kings 11:31–34, 38), whom he regards as the first of the 'opposition prophets'. Nevertheless, in the person of Ahijah the qualities of the mantic seer and of the messenger of God, are combined.
27. Greenberg, "Religion" (1979), p. 111 points out that victory prophecies such as Elisha's (2 Kings 13:14–19), and Jonah ben Amittai's (2 Kings 14:25–26) produced a new idea: a saviour king who would restore the kingdom to its former grandeur. Thus 'Messianic' hopes were placed on kings of the northern kingdom much earlier than on the House of David.
28. On the other hand, there seems to be no magic element in Elisha's striking the Arameans with blindness, since in this story Elisha prays to God in each of its three parts, 2 Kings 6:17, 18 and 20.
29. For a more elaborate discussion see Rofé, *Stories* (1988), pp. 58–60; 132–135.

supplement the picture of relations that prevailed between prophets and kings in the Northern Kingdom.[30]

The Historical Connection

The characteristics of the man of God make the stories in which he figures belong to the sphere of legend. Their inclusion in the frame of historiography does not seem to have been given adequate treatment, from the literary standpoint.[31]

It is worth pausing here to consider a case in which one can point to the formation of a link that connects legend and Deuteronomistic historiography.[32] Ahijah the Shilonite is a man of God who embodies the characteristics enumerated above. Although this is not explicitly stated, he is associated with healing: "he will tell you what shall happen to the child" (1 Kings 14:3); his appearance contains elements of surprise and enigma (vs. 6); and he gives the wife of Jeroboam a sign (vs. 11). But he is also the man who delivers a speech with a clear Deuteronomistic component[33] that includes a reference to the house of David: "and tore the kingdom away from the house of David and gave it to you..." (1 Kings 14:8). However, it is the context of this declaration that is more important for our purposes. His opening words to Jeroboam are "Because I exalted you from among the people, and made you leader over my people Israel..." (1 Kings 14:7); and the explanation of the reason for the punishment begins: "...and yet you have not been like my servant David" (vs. 8). The use of David as a criterion for good and evil is a

30. Uffenheimer, "Policy" (1955); Reviv, *Clan* (1979), pp. 189–195.

31. Fairy tale being the English equivalent of the *Gattung* called *Märchen* in German. For its classical categorization see Gunkel, *Märchen* (1917); *Genesis* (1964), pp. VII-XXVI; *Legends* (1966); Coats, *Saga* (1985).
Concerning legends and vitae see also Rofé, *Stories* (1988), p. 41.

32. Noth, *Studien* (1943), pp. 87–90; *D History* (1981), pp. 75–78 differentiates between the Dtr. as writer, and as redactor.

33. On the form and function of orations in the Deuteronomistic composition see Weinfeld, *Deuteronomy* (1972), pp. 10–58.

recurrent, almost central component of the Deuteronomistic approach and many scholars have discussed its significance.[34] But the expressions 'I have raised you above the people,' and 'made you נגיד (prince) over the people of Israel' recall the prophecy of Nathan: "I took you from the pasture, from following the sheep, that you should be נגיד (prince) over my people Israel" (2 Sam. 7:8). The full meaning of the connection between these words may become apparent after an analysis of certain points:

a) The formulary nature of the opening sentence "Because I exalted you from among the people, and made you leader over my people Israel" (1 Kings 14:7) is clearly apparent: "יען (because)...", "נגיד (prince)"[35] which appear twice more in similar declarations to a king (2 Sam. 7:8 and 1 Kings 16:2).[36]

34. Von Rad claims that the Deuteronomist uses David as a measuring rod for the kings of Judah, and asserts that "their heart was not perfect (whole) with God" like David's (1 Kings 8:61; 11:4; 15:3–4), thus bringing disaster on the kingdom. But the king was not responsible for the cultic life of the people, nor does the book of Deuteronomy, which regards kingship on the whole as a concession to reality, make such demands on that office.
The Deuteronomist was the first to combine two initially independent, one could almost say mutually exclusive, traditions of election — the Covenant with Israel (connected with Moses and the Exodus), and the covenant with David (1 Kings 8:25; 9:5). Through this fusion the Deuteronomist is able to put into the mouths of the kings of Judah a claim that God ought to keep his promises, not only to David, but also to Moses (1 Kings 8:15, 34, 36, 53, 56). Thus the king becomes responsible, in the eyes of the Deuteronomist, for the country's adhering to the laws of Moses. In other words, to the people's "heart being perfect with God." Von Rad, *Theologie* (1958), vol. 1 pp. 336–337; *Theology* (1962), vol. 1 pp. 337–338.

35. For the meaning of נגיד see Chapter Four p. 83. Liver, "Nagid" (1968); Hasel, "Nagid" (1984), both with further bibliography.

36. When Ahijah addresses Jeroboam in a speech about kingship, he applies to Rehoboam (and possibly to all his descendants) the title נשיא, thus limiting the scope of his authority (1 Kings 11:34). See Montgomery, *Kings* (1951), p. 243; Gray, *Kings* (1964), p. 275.

b) Variations appear in the three Deuteronomistic passages:
1. To David — "I took you from the pasture" (2 Sam. 7:8).
2. To Jeroboam — "I exalted you from among the people" (1 Kings 14:8).
3. To Baasha — "I exalted you out of the dust" (1 Kings 16:2).

These three verses form an intentional gradation (pasture being the highest, and dust the lowest, see also pp. 88–89). In my opinion, it may allude to God's attitude towards the kings of the North, as compared with His attitude towards David. Moreover it emphasizes the deterioration in His attitude from the first step towards dividing the kingdom, i.e., the anointing of Jeroboam,[37] to the third king of the North; in other words, the change for the worse from Jeroboam to Baasha.

c) Other parts of the prophecy of Ahijah in 1 Kings 14 also contain allusions to Nathan's prophecy in 2 Sam. 7.

ניר לדוד (a lamp for David) — Ahijah's words to Jeroboam contain an implied condition: "Yet to his son I will give one tribe, that David my servant may always have a lamp before me" (1 Kings 11:36). The reference to the lamp recurs in the Deuteronomistic explanation of what happens to Abijam: "Nevertheless for David's sake the Lord his God gave him a lamp in Jerusalem" (1 Kings 15:4), and also in the remark about Joram: "Yet the Lord would not destroy Judah, for the sake of David his servant, since he promised to give a lamp to him and to his sons for ever" (2 Kings 8:19).

Another expression, **בית נאמן** (a sure house) also appears in the conditional promise to Jeroboam: "And if you will hearken... I will be with you, and will build you a sure house..." (1 Kings 11:38), and this brings us directly back to Nathan's prophecy (2 Sam. 7:16).

37. For instance Noth, "Jerusalem" (1950) points out that the Dtr. justifies the political split while condemning the cultic one.

This is noteworthy because the phrase בית נאמן is so rare, appearing only in 1 Sam. 25:28 in connection with David, in 1 Sam. 2:35 in connection with the functions of the priest before God's anointed, and in a similar context about Moses in Num. 12:7.

d) The formulary cross-reference between the Northern Kingdom and the Kingdom of Judah in the Deuteronomistic history, appears only at certain points: (a) at the first stages of the divided monarchy, up to and including the third king of the North — Baasha, and then sporadically in (b) 2 Kings 8:19[38] and (c) in the epilogue of the Deuteronomistic writer in 2 Kings 17: 7–23, esp. vss. 18, 19 and 21. In other words: once the fact of the two separate kingdoms, the north and the south, was firmly established, the Deuteronomist no longer felt the need for such cross references.

We can now draw the following conclusions: a) There is an almost identical formulation of the central ideas in the legends and the Deuteronomistic speeches, to the point where one may speak of conscious intent on the part of the editor-author; in other words, for him the two are closely connected; both serve his hortatory objectives and were for him of equal importance.[39] Thus the inclusion of legends in the Deuteronomistic historiography[40] is certainly not the result of a random collection of material.

38. It has often been pointed out that the Dtr. writer, for reasons of his own, turns the dynasty of Ahab into a completely negative symbol — far more than would be justified by history, e.g., Eichrodt, *Theologie* vol. 1 (1948), pp. 223–224; *Theology* (1961), pp. 441–442.

39. I totally agree with the statement that the biblical author is generally more interested in the moral of the story than in the accuracy of the historical facts. Nevertheless the editors left whole blocks in which the factual informative aspect overwhelms the descriptive mode. Cf. Zakovitch, "Story" (1983); Whybray, *Succession* (1968), pp. 62–65, 71–75.

40. When using the term 'pure historiography' in the biblical context, I have two points in mind: a. from the point of contents the writer's interest is only in events on the public level, even when he now and again describes occurences in which only one (or a few) characters participate. b. in 'pure

b) The editor-author[41] portrays a different cultic (one is almost tempted to say religious) situation in the Northern Kingdom from that of the Southern Kingdom. This difference is apparent in ritual, above all in Jeroboam's golden calves at Beth-el and Dan,[42] and in turning to alien gods e.g., Baalzebub (2 Kings 1). However, it seems to me that the difference is no less apparent in the characteristic activity of the northern man of God: the mysterious element in his appearance, the unpredictability that can make contact with him dangerous.

Particularly outstanding cases are: the story of Elijah and the three captains of fifty who approached him disrespectfully

historiography' the reporting mode is more prominent than the descriptive or scenaric mode.

41. By 'author' I mean the person responsible for forming the early stratum of the story, and by 'editor' the person who is responsible for its present place in the text. Where it is virtually certain that the editor is also responsible for the details of literary shape — I will use the term the editor-author, i.e., he interferes with the sequence of events, by placing stories in an order which seems unreasonable even according to biblical standards; he uses special literary devices or adds reflective remarks.
As for the time of composition: it would seem that the final redaction of at least some of the stories is very late indeed, from the Persian Period. For the general attitude and its justification see Rofé, "Rebekah" (1976), and more recently Rofé, "David" (1986), esp. pp. 62–64.

42. Noth, "Jerusalem" (1950) is of the opinion that 1 Kings 11:29–39, 12:1–20, 26–31 and 14:1–18, all come from northern sources. The passages reflect the situation in the north and express the attitude of the northern tribes towards Jerusalem although the editor-author considers Jeroboam's establishment of a separate cult a mistake (see 1 Kings 14:8–16).
Von Rad, *Theologie* (1958), vol. 1 p. 66; *Theology* (1962), vol. 1 pp. 58–59, thinks that from a point of view of cult, Jeroboam does not rebel against the accepted practices: the calves, he maintains, are not a revolutionary innovation, but merely an expression of the concepts prevailing in the north. They are only symbols, and the sanctuaries Jeroboam built are temples for YHWH.
In this case the views of von Rad seem more appropriate than that of Haran, *Temples* (1978), pp. 28–30 (esp. note 28); 90–92, who considers the calves to be symbols of popular worship, as against the esoteric symbols of the Jerusalem cult.

(2 Kings 1:9–17); the children torn apart by bears because they mocked Elisha (2 Kings 2:23–24); the magical element in Elisha's deeds (2 Kings 4) and his being known as one who can cure the sick (2 Kings 5) and perform miracles (2 Kings 2).

None of these characteristics appears in descriptions connected with the Southern Kingdom before the destruction of Samaria, and in earlier descriptions, of the united monarchy, they appear only in connection with Saul, not with David. No such characteristic actions appear in any of the stories about Samuel in connection with David. Had the same editor edited all the historiographic books of the Former Prophets,[43] he must have been aware of a difference in the religious climate of the Northern Kingdom.[44] But even if it was not the same editor, a different religious reality still emerges from the stories themselves.

A Wrathful God

God on the one hand has a close relationship with David, but he also reveals himself in violent outbursts of destructive fury and incomprehensible wrath, whose causes are mentioned but not explained.[45] There are also manifestations of divine intervention in

43. For a definition of 'editor' see note 41; on the question of authorship of the book of Kings see note 14.
44. The special religious climate of the Northern Kingdom is better understood against the background of the general differences between North and South, such as kingship. See Alt, "Königtum" (1951), "Monarchy" (1968); Noth, "Gott, König, Volk" (1950).
45. Eichrodt, *Theologie* (1948), vol. 1 pp. 124–131; *Theology* (1961), vol. 1 pp. 258–266 holds that wrath is only one facet of the deity, whose enduring characteristics are love and justice. Eichrodt points to late biblical texts, where the distinction is clear: wrath is confined for sinners and God's enemies (Psalms 69:25, 28; Daniel 9:16). Eichrodt also points to texts that represent God's wrath as unusual, caused by people's bad behaviour: Genesis 6:1; 1 Sam. 15:11; Amos 7:1–6.
In my study, however, the problem of God's wrath arises only when no sufficient explanation for it is provided in the text. Eichrodt maintains that in

favour of David which are somewhat obscure. Thus two religious attitudes appear in the Book of Samuel.

One is represented by Nathan's speech (2 Sam. 7), which states that God will punish David "when he commits iniquity" (vs. 14). The chastisement, however, will be of limited severity: "I will chasten him with the rod of men, with the stripes of the sons of men" (vs. 14).[46] We are thus faced with an extreme manifestation of the divine concept of morality, as God's reactions are explained rationally, and are even announced in advance.[47]

The second attitude shows God acting with no warning and no explanation whatsoever. This is dramatically portrayed in the killing of Uzzah for placing his hand on the Ark (2 Sam. 6:6–7) and by the plague that followed the census (2 Sam. 24). The extreme nature of the latter is stressed in the opening words: "Again the anger of the Lord was kindled against Israel" (2 Sam. 24:1). These stories will be dicussed in Chapters One and Two below.

The answer God gives David about the battle in the Valley of Rephaim, also includes a mysterious element: "And when you hear the sound of marching in the tops of the balsam trees, then bestir

the Bible no capricious tyranny or demonic fury is ever attributed to the deity. He arrives at this conclusion by comparing the behaviour of the God of Israel with that of the pagan religions. Eichrodt makes the point that the God of Israel never reaches the degree of hatred and jealousy of the Babylonian or Greek gods, thus his point is relative. For a full treatment of the subject see Dunston, The Dark Side (1983).

It is worth noting the attitude of Labuschange, *Incomparability* (1966), that the incomparability and mysteriousness of God, constitute the essence of His uniqueness, and it is for these qualities that he is worshipped, as can be seen by expressions such as "who is like thee" or "and who is like me" (Exodus 15:11; Deuteronomy 3:24; Isaiah 44:7; Jeremiah 49:19; Micah 7:18; Psalms 35:10; 71:19; 89:9 (MT); 113:5).

46. For a more detailed discussion of 2 Sam. 7:14 see below Chapter Four, pp. 98–99 & note 75.

47. Otto, *Heilige* (1927), pp. 1–22; 43–57; *Holy* (1969), pp. 1–19; 50–59.

yourself; for then the Lord has gone out before you to smite the army of the Philistines" (2 Sam. 5:24). Although the formulation is abstruse,[48] it seems to me quite clear that the reference is not to a military stratagem that David himself could have executed, but to divine assistance involving a miraculous element.[49] It may be that the instruction is given in rather vague terms because this is typical of the language of oracles.[50]

However, between 2 Sam. 6 and 24, we find no further manifestations of this kind. From the Uzzah episode and bringing of the Ark up to Jerusalem, to the purchase of Araunah the Jebusite's threshing-floor where the plague was stopped, there is no mention of the Lord's wrathful outbursts. In 2 Sam. 7–23 there is nothing mysterious or irrational in the encounters with the Lord. In all the literary material dealing with the kingdom of David, from the moment he was made king over all of Israel we meet only the first attitude, i.e., the one portrayed in Nathan's speech.

I have no intention of questioning the conventional approach that looks upon 2 Sam. 9–20 and 1 Kings 1–2 as a single literary unit.[51] But it seems to me that the placing of these stories — the

48. The Medieval commentators tend to stress the direct intervention of God in the course of events and treat it as a miracle, by emphasizing its ideological aspect. For example: "As the Philistines were approaching, the Israelites beheld them when they were no more than four cubits away. The Israelites said to David: why are we standing still? And David said: I was ordered from heaven to do nothing until the treetops begin to stir... Immediately thereafter the treetops began to move and they attacked them... And the Lord said to the מלאכי השרת [= archangels] see the difference between David and Saul..." The reference is most probably to Saul's behaviour at Michmash, 1 Sam. 13, and his attempt to excuse it (vss. 11–12). *Midrash Shoher Tov Psalm 27 and Pesikta Rabbati 88.*
49. Licht, "Miracle" (1968).
50. See above note 4.
51. Since Rost, *Thronnachfolge* (1926), 2 Sam. 9–20 and 1 Kings 1–2 have been regarded as one literary unit. Recently this assumption has been questioned, see for example Bar Efrat, "Succession" (1983); and cf. Kaufmann, "David" (1957).

bringing up of the Ark and the stopping of the plague, at the beginning and at the end of this section respectively, endows them with an additional dimension. I shall endeavour to explain these matters in the detailed discussion in the following chapters.

David's Plan and the Divine Plan

Perusal of the first eight chapters of the Second Book of Samuel[52] leads one to ponder on the fundamental principle behind the writing and the interlacing of these chapters. It seems to me that from several standpoints they can be regarded as a separate literary unit within the court history, although they are not usually designated as such. A detailed discussion of this issue is not in place here, but it should be noted that the sequence in which the events are reported is not necessarily dictated by chronological order. This is usually pointed out with relation to the order of events in 2 Sam. 5, according to which the conquest of Jerusalem preceded the decisive victory over the Philistines. Most modern commentators agree that the victory must have come first, because had David not defeated the Philistines, he would have been unable to assault Jerusalem.[53]

Likewise, it is usually assumed that the opening of 2 Sam. 7, which includes the comment: "and the Lord had given him rest from all his enemies round about" (vs. 1) is more appropriate to a later stage in David's career.[54] Moreover, it seems reasonable to assume that he would have bought Araunah's threshing-floor before he expressed his desire to build a house for God. But this

52. In my opinion 2 Sam. 1–8 constitutes a separate literary unit. For a detailed treatment see Gelander, Relations (1984).
53. Budde, *Samuelbücher* (1902), pp. 218 ff.; Hertzberg, *Samuelbücher* (1960), p. 221; *Samuel* (1964), p. 265; Ward, David's Rise (1967), pp. 181–184; Grønbaek, *Aufstieg* (1971), p. 251; Reviv, *Clan* (1979), pp. 124–125; Garsiel, *David* (1975), pp. 41–46. See also the discussion below, Chapter Five, pp. 112–113.
54. See Hertzberg, *Samuelbücher* (1960), pp. 232–233; *Samuel* (1964), p. 284; McCarthy, "Deuteronomistic History" (1965).

transaction is not recorded until 2 Sam. 24 (see Chapter Two below).

The manner of selecting and interweaving the accounts of the various events, is designed to prompt the message. One example is the arrangement of the herald scene in 2 Sam. 1. Here David wants to make it clear that the king of Israel is not a ruler like all others, but "the Lord's anointed", with all this entails. It is surprising that David sentences the Amalekite to death after having him executed (note the position of vs. 16 after vs. 15!), and he then goes on to explain the reason for doing so. In this way the phrase "the Lord's anointed" is emphasized by being the last words uttered in this scene. Even the final interrogation and execution of the Amalekite are described after the people had "mourned and wept and fasted until evening for Saul and for Jonathan his son and for the people of the Lord..." (vs. 12), during which time the Amalekite seems to have been forgotten. This peculiar sequence seems to be designed in order to strengthen the impression that the mourning is spontaneous. In my opinion the order of events, as they really happened, was different.[55]

The following stages of David's enterprises portray the establishment of his kingdom as the fulfilment of a divine plan. This plan was designed to establish a kingdom which the Lord would protect and guide, while the kingdom would carry out his wishes.[56] The fact that David became king over all Israel, despite all

55. It is reasonable to suppose that the questioning of the Amalekite was completed in a single hearing and that it was only after he was put to death that the fasting, weeping and eulogizing commenced. But according to the story the mourning interrupted the investigation. Likewise I would assume that David's judgement "your blood be upon your head" (vs. 16) must have been delivered before the execution rather than after it. Ehrlich, *Mikra ki-Pheschuto* (1900), vol. 2 p. 181 interprets vs. 16 as accentuating the holiness of God's anointed, who must not be harmed. Thus David is protecting himself, because now he is God's anointed. See also North, "Kingship" (1932).

56. With regard to the concept of "the kingdom of God" I tend to accept the view

obstacles,[57] must lead to the conclusion that this was the will of God.[58] Indeed, the text finds ways of indicating that David himself realized that he owed his success to God. This is particularly conspicuous in the arrangement of 2 Sam. 5. In the opinion of the editor-author it is this realization that ensures the stability of David's rule and will secure the perpetuation of his house. In other words, it may be said that the central message of these chapters should be gleaned from the very choice, structure and organization of the material. The message is that David's kingship is based on a 'mutual guarantee' between him and the Lord: David's declared faith guarantees his rule, and his rule is a guarantee of adherence to everlasting faith.

that according to the Second Book of Samuel it is the basis and core of David's activity, and that it does not precede the establishment of his reign. This is no place for a discussion of this concept. But Buber *Königtum Gottes* (1932), pp. 3–12 maintains that the "kingdom of God" is earlier, referring to Gideon's speech (Jud. 8:23), and Eichrodt, *Theologie* (1948), vol. 1 pp. 90 ff.; *Theology* (1961), vol. 1 pp. 194 ff., believes that this concept goes as far back as the period of the desert wanderings.

57. It is customary to see in Joab's killing of Abner a deed extremely damaging to David's efforts, his immediate political intentions and his long-range plans, one that made his future uncertain. Hertzberg, *Samuelbücher* (1960), pp. 208–214; *Samuel* (1964), pp. 254–262; Ward, David's Rise (1967), p. 160; Grønbaek, *Aufstieg* (1971), p. 236; et al.
The notion that the Lord guided events in favour of David is very clearly enunciated by the medieval commentators. See Rabbi Levi ben Gershom: "And now God, blessed be his name, turned events so as to bring about a quarrel between Abner and Ishboshet, and therefore Abner attempted to crown David as the king of all Israel, since the kingdom came to him from the Lord, and it is to be expected that he was not unaware that Michal was not defiled by Palti ben Laish." In this way Ralbag is trying to resolve two difficulties at once: why do Abner and Ishboshet quarrel, and how can a woman who was married to another return to her former husband — cf. Dt. 24:1–3.

58. In 2 Sam. 4 two episodes are combined — the story of Mephiboshet and the story of Ishboshet's murder. This combination leads to the conclusion that the events were directed by God. The whole chapter paints a picture of general weakness in the house of Saul. Rashi comments: "He keeps thinking how the kingdom was slipping away from the house of Saul." Kimhi says: "To make it

Very little is known of the overall content of this faith. Where the House of David is concerned studies of the history of biblical faith usually deal only with specific subjects relating to historical developments.[59] But it seems to me that the establishment of David's kingdom resulted in a series of changes in religious concepts whose implications extended far beyond the administrative field. These changes, therefore, are not only a turning-point; they can be called revolutionary,[60] especially in their understanding of God's character and His ways, and the relationship between Him and human beings. It may be reasonably assumed that such a revolution, with its manifold projections, is not only the result of David's activities,[61] but that the editor-author wanted to attribute it to him.[62] My study focuses only on those chapters in the Second Book of Samuel and a few additional texts directly relevant to this theme.

known that after the death of Ishboshet the house of Saul contained no successor worthy of the kingdom." Most modern commentators agree.

59. Von Rad, "Zelt" (1931); "Tent" (1966); Alt "Königtum" (1951); "Monarchy" (1968); Noth, "Jerusalem" (1950); "Gott, König, Volk" (1950).

60. Von Rad, *Theologie* (1958), vol. 1 pp. 36–68; *Theology* (1962), vol. 1 pp. 44–75, believes that the establishment of the kingdom revolutionized many aspects of life, but he argues that the roots of this revolution lie in the more distant past. He deals mainly with phenomena related to the individual's relationship with the community, and maintains that a characteristic of the period preceeding the kingdom was the feeling of each individual that he belonged to the community, with no barrier or tension. Every event was regarded as occurring to the whole community rather than to an individual, and life was organized around the cultic rites. The establishment of the kingdom brought about a change that was most apparent in the disappearance of this sense of belonging.

61. It is reasonable to suppose that changes in the religious concept expressed in legislation were the result of reforms, such as that of Jehoshaphat (especially if we accept the description in 2 Chron. 17:7–9; 19:1–11), or of Hezekiah (2 Chron. 29–31). See also Eichrodt, *Theologie* vol. 1 (1948), pp. 25–40; *Theology* vol. 1 (1961), pp. 70–99.

62. Greenberg, "Religion" (1979) thinks that the Israelite religion is based on a folk religion of a unique character, and that its main forms of expression and institutions were established long before the kingship.

CHAPTER ONE

BRINGING THE ARK UP TO JERUSALEM — THE MEANING OF THE UZZAH INCIDENT (2 Sam. 6)

According to the order of the chapters in the Second Book of Samuel, bringing the Ark up to Jerusalem was David's first significant act, after his decisive victory over the Philistines.[1] According to the order of events in the Book of Chronicles, this was his very first act following the capture of Jerusalem.[2]

As is well known, the story of bringing up the Ark is connected with two episodes: the Uzzah incident and the story of Michal. As to the former, we read that as the Ark was being brought out of the house of Abinadab, Uzzah, who was driving the cart together with his brother Ahio, stretched out his hand and took hold of the Ark "for the oxen stumbled" (2 Sam. 6:6). This kindled the Lord's

1. It is generally accepted that the order of events was different from the one in the present text, and that the capture of Jerusalem was made possible only after the victory over the Philistines. See already Budde, *Samuelbücher* (1902), pp. 70, 218, 224; *Samuel* (1894), pp. 81, 83; for a review of the different approaches see Ward, David's Rise (1967); Reviv, *Clan* (1979), pp. 123–124. McCarter, *II Samuel* (1984), pp. 174 ff. following Hertzberg, ascribes the present order of the events in 2 Sam. 5:11–8:18 to the Deuteronomistic editor, whose main purpose was to emphasize the election of David and of Jerusalem by the Lord.
2. The list of the mighty men among the Israelites who now decided to join David (1 Chron. 11:10–12:41) is placed between two major events: the capture of Jerusalem and the bringing up of the Ark. This emphasizes the interest of the Chronicler in establishing the fact that all the tribes participated in bringing up the Ark. (cf. 2 Sam. 5–6 with 1 Chron. 11–13. See also Japhet, *Chronicles H* (1977), pp. 228–237; *Chronicles ET* (1989), pp. 270–278.

anger against Uzzah, and He struck him dead. David, enraged by this, refused to bring the Ark to Jerusalem. Instead, he took it into the house of Obed-edom the Gittite, where it remained for three months and brought blessings upon Obed-edom and his household. Only then did David bring the Ark up to Jerusalem.

The Michal episode describes Michal's contemptuous reaction as she saw David "leaping and dancing before the Lord" (2 Sam. 6:16). Compare this with the Chronicler's variant, which describes the event in milder terms: "King David dancing and making merry" (1 Chr. 15:29). David rebukes her in strong language, and she "had no child to the day of her death" (2 Sam. 6:23).

There is no general agreement among scholars whether the two episodes originally belonged to our story. Those who consider the Uzzah incident to be the primary one, regard the Michal story as superfluous, and therefore a secondary addition;[3] others think the exact opposite.[4]

The final redaction of 2 Sam. 6 is clearly tendentious. The beginning of the chapter[5] leads to the assumption that the story

3. According to Rost, *Thronnachfolge* (1926); *Succession* (1982), it is here in 2 Sam. 6 that the succession narrative begins. Von Rad, *Theologie* (1958), vol. 1 p. 310; *Theology* (1962), vol.1 pp. 312–313 too, believes that introducing the scene with Michal, because of the motif of barrenness, turns one's attention to the question of who will inherit David's throne.
4. Such as Hempel, *Geschichten* (1964), p. 148.
5. The idea that the opening of this chapter was originally part of a different story is based: a) on the word "again" [עוד], which appears in 2 Sam. 6:1 (MT); b) on the phrase "all the chosen men of Israel", which seems to fit a military context. In addition to the general meaning of the expression, which includes all young men (Eccl. 11:9); see the many times this word is parallel to 'virgin' (Deut. 32:25; Is. 23:4; Jer. 51:22 etc.), or the more specific one of "the chosen one" (1 Sam. 9:2; Num. 11:28 etc.), the expression appears very frequently in a military context: 2 Sam. 10:9; 2 Chron. 36:17; Amos 4:10; Is. 31:8; 40:30; Jer. 48:15; 49:26; 50:30; 51:22; Ez. 23:23; Psalms 78:31; Proverbs 20:29; Lament. 1:15 etc. and c) on the large number of 30,000 (in LXX 70,000).

was cut off from some other story — either the story of the census and the Araunah threshing floor (2 Sam. 24),[6] or a now lost account of a military campaign during which the Ark was rescued.[7] If this assumption is correct, then the story was deliberately cut-off from any other event, in order to emphasize its specific purpose — praise of David. Scholars usually stress the parallel between the story of the Ark as related in 1 Sam. 4–6 and in 2 Sam. 6, some of them think that the narratives were deliberately designed to accentuate the analogy through contrast.[8] This interpretation sees the main purpose of the narrative as extolling the virtues of David by indirect criticism of the House of Saul. This latter perception leads to viewing the story of Michal as the main focus, since it also contains a sly dig at the House of Saul (in David's statement: "It was before the Lord, who chose me above your father, and above all his house...", 2 Sam. 6:21).

6. Carlson, *David* (1964), pp. 62–76; Auerbach, *Wüste* (1938), vol. 1 {6} p. 221.
7. Budde, *Samuelbücher* (1902), p. 227; *Samuel* (1894), pp. 81–82; Blenkinsopp, "Kiriath-Jearim" (1969).
8. Some scholars consider the stories of the Ark in the First and Second Books of Samuel to be two separate narratives, from two different sources: the first from Mitzpah and the second from "David's Source". So for example Bleek, *Einleitung* (1878), pp. 222–223; Lotz, "Bundeslade" (1901).
As against this Kittel, *Geschichte* (1923), pp. 187 ff. points to the likeness of the two stories, while Steuernagel, *Lehrbuch* (1912), pp. 332–335 agreeing with Gressman, *Geschichtsschreibung* (1910), pp. 11–13, 233–234 holds that the two stories have a common origin.
Tur Sinai, *Peschuto* vol. 2 (1964), pp. 134–136 and following him McCarter, *II Samuel* (1984), p. 184 hypothesizes that the story relating "And he slew some of the men of Beth Shemesh" and the story about Uzzah are two different versions of one aetiological narrative (1 Sam. 6 especially 12–15 and vs. 19).
The survey by McCarter, *II Samuel* (1984), pp. 182–184, stresses mainly the fact that, of late, scholars have voiced reservations about the two stories being actually one (1 Sam. 4–6 and 2 Sam. 6), pointing to the lack of correspondence in details. In his opinion, the best proof that the stories are independent is that they belong to two distinct categories of surviving ancient Near Eastern literature.

The Uzzah Episode

Anyone focusing his attention on the Uzzah incident must realize its mainly theological significance. The Jewish commentators maintain that David learned his lesson from the sin he committed. That sin (or sins) is explained in various ways.

Abrabanel lists four different sins. Yosef Kara, followed by Kimhi, says: "Since it was the Levites who had to carry the Ark on their shoulders." Some commentators speak of the sin being twofold: the Ark was jolted around in a wagon rather than carried on the shoulders; and furthermore, it was carried by foreigners, not Levites.[9] The introduction of the Levites at this point is certainly anachronisitc[10] and is mentioned here only to demonstrate how far some commentators have gone in search of sins.[11]

Kaufmann, on the other hand, finds no sin at all here. According to him, "David wished to turn the symbol of wrath into the new symbol of eternal grace... There is still great anxiety about the Ark... but David's will is stronger than his fear, and therefore the wrath of God finally turns into a blessing."[12]

9. Malkiel, "Ark" (1962), esp. p. 126.
10. For the differences in views between the early historiography and the Chronicler as to the function and essence of the Levites, see Noth, *Geschichtsbild* (1930) pp. 98 ff.; *C History* (1981), pp. 75 ff.; Gunneweg, *Leviten* (1965), pp. 204–215.
    For an explanation of the Levites' role, see Milgrom, *Terminology* (1970), pp. 16–28.
11. Campbell "Ark" (1979) maintains that the purpose of the story is to emphasize that returning the Ark is beyond David's power and is not under his control. Only after the Lord gives a sign of His assent will the Ark return. Campbell thinks that the story was split up to show that a new era had begun in Jerusalem. But, in his opinion, 2 Sam. 6 was written in a different context from that of the story in 1 Sam. 4–6, even though the author knew of the existence of the latter and was influenced by it.
12. Kaufmann, *Religion* (1947), p. 169.

In my opinion, the chapter in its present form gives equal weight to both episodes. If one of the two was a more recent addition as the story was taking shape, it is difficult to decide which. An analysis of the structure of the narrative and the way it was formed indicates the unity of the chapter, as will be shown later. In order to comprehend the story's full significance I see no way of avoiding an analysis of the Michal episode. But the Uzzah episode is of greater importance in the context of the present study, so I shall deal with it first.[13]

David's bringing the Ark to Jerusalem was undoubtedly, at least in part, a political act.[14] Noth, Clements and others believe that it

13. On 2 Sam. 6 as the beginning of the tradition of Mount Zion as the Mountain of God (Psalms 46, 48 and 76), see Rohland, Erwählungstradition (1956). However, von Rad, *Theologie* (1958), vol. 1 p. 53; *Theology* vol. 1 (1962), p. 45 accepts the Scandinavian approach that the story in 2 Sam. 6 no longer relates to a single historical event, but rather to an annual religious rite, such as we read about in 1 Kings 8, and the similar tradition that appears in Psalm 132. This is the basis for the concept of the royal festival of Zion. see also, Eichrodt, *Theologie* (1948) vol. 1 pp. 44–81; *Theology* (1961), vol. 1 pp. 107–177, esp. 122–126 and bibliography there.

14. Noth, "Jerusalem" (1950), pp. 174, 181 ff. believes that the relationship of Israel to Jerusalem as the holy city stems only from the power of the Ark, because of the long tradition associated with it, even though in time, the holiness of the Temple lost all connection with the Ark.
Jeremias, "Lade" (1971) also claims that without the Ark, one cannot imagine the creation of the 'Davidic tradition'. We read in Jer. 3:16: "And when you have multiplied and increased in the land, in those days, says the Lord, they shall no more say, 'The Ark of the covenant of the Lord.' It shall not come to mind, or be remembered, or missed; it shall not be made again." He finds evidence, although of a later date, of the tradition of the Ark being replaced by the tradition of the chosen city, Jerusalem and Zion. Unlike Smend, *Jahwekrieg* (1966); *Jahwe War* (1970), he does not think that the tradition of the Ark and its functions were completely eliminated with the development of the Jerusalem-Zion tradition. Compare with von Rad, *Theologie* (1958) vol. 1 p. 52; *Theology* (1962), vol. 1 pp. 44–45, who thinks that had David failed to bring the Ark up to Jerusalem, the Temple and its ritual would have been nothing more than the private possession of the House of David.

was an attempt to establish his connection with older traditions represented symbolically by the Ark. By bringing the Ark to his city, David may be seen as accepting ancient cult symbols,[15] whether tribal or intertribal, and thereby appearing to be perpetuating the tradition. In other words, "David is bringing Shiloh to Jerusalem."[16] According to this interpretation he must have taken

On the connection between religion and politics, with special emphasis on the religious aspect as the main characteristic of the Judean kingdom, see Eichrodt, *Theologie* (1948), vol. 1 pp. 222–230; *Theology* (1961), vol. 1, pp. 439, 442–456. For a survey of this subject, see Kegler, *Politisches Geschehen,* (1977). On the difficulties in defining the precise functions of the Ark, see Schmitt, *Zelt* (1972), pp. 49–174 and bibliography there.

15. In the opinion of Noth, *System* (1930), pp. 66, 95 ff.; the Ark fulfilled an important function in the crisis involved in the conquest and settlement of the land: the desert God was not easily acceptable in a land of permanent, concrete local deities. For this reason the Ark, embodying the actual presence of the Lord, was of great significance. This factor gains importance by the presence of tribes which were not involved in the Mount Sinai tradition. To them, the Ark became the representative of the Lord as a national deity. Cf. Clements, *David* (1967), p. 53.

    As against this, Jeremias, "Lade" (1971), argues that Bible research has not come up with any definite information as to the nomadic past of the Ark; nor is it clear whether it came to be considered sacred only upon settlement in the Land.

    Von Rad, "Zelt" (1931); "Tent" (1966) describes stages in the concept of the Ark and its functioning, which are expressed differently in the various sources: The concept of the Ark as connected with an oracle conflicts with its concept as the throne of the Deity, whereas defining it as the Ark of the Covenant is the result of the Deuteronomist's blending the two concepts. But representing the cherubs as defenders of the Ark is a later Priestly addition, in the attempt to bridge the gap between the tradition of the Tabernacle and the traditions of the Ark.

    On the other hand, Milgrom, *Terminology* (1970), p. 69, maintains that in the biblical tradition, there is no distinction between the Tabernacle and the Ark. For a survey of the traditions of the Ark as expressed in the Deuteronomistic accounts, see Fretheim "Ark" (1968). His hypothesis is that the Ark continued to serve as a ritual object until the reforms of Josiah.

16. Bentzen, "Ark" (1948); Eissfeldt, *Einleitung* (1956), pp. 156 ff.; *Introduction* (1965), pp. 143 ff.; Carslon, *David* (1964), passim.

this step to allay fears and reduce tension. The fact that it was necessary for him to make such a demonstration to stress his promise to maintain the sacred tradition, shows that there must have been a great deal of apprehension as to what effect David and his deeds might have on that tradition.[17]

In any event, it was not the intention of the author to impute any grave sin to David,[18] and especially not in connection with the bringing up of the Ark. Insofar as what he did was defined as sin it was only an expression of the tensions arising from his actions, tensions that the author of the chapter wished to dispel. It is reasonable to assume that opposition to cultic changes along with political and administrative changes came from conservative elements clinging to the old order. However, these are mere suppositions, and I have no way of substantiating them.

As to perceiving the narrative as a cultic story relating in some way to a temple festival, or the so-called Royal Zion Festival,[19]

17. It is worth noting the words of Eichrodt, *Theologie* (1948), vol. 1 p. 224; *Theology* (1961), vol. 1 p. 442: "The more men were accustomed to see Yahweh's working in the form of unexpected interventions in the course of events, of explosive acts of power shattering in their force, the less they were inclined to acknowledge as the principal champion of the Yahweh religion a man who held office quite without reference to these divine operations."
18. It is hard to agree that in this context 'the anger' has the same meaning as in other formulae. McCarthy, "Deuteronomistic History" (1965), lists ten places where 'the anger' is connected with abandoning the ways of the Lord, but 2 Sam 6–7 is not among them.
19. Some of the hypotheses on this subject do not appear to me to be well grounded. Carlson, *David* (1964), pp. 60 ff.; 190 ff. believes that the story contains elements parallel to the epic of Kereth, particularly in vss. 11–13, where he finds a parallel with the six-day march to "UDM RBT". He thinks the name "Obed-edom" is based on theophoric elements identical with UDM RBT, where Kereth went to look for a wife. For the text see: Ginsberg, *Keret* (1946), pp. 16, 38; cf. *ANET* p. 144 who translates "Udum the Grand". North, "Kingship" (1932), relates the text of 2 Sam. 6 to the royal festival of Zion, which celebrated the Lord's choice of Zion as his domicile.

I have no means of ascertaining the existence of pre-Israeli cult elements that may have been absorbed into the story.

It is possible that certain elements have become merely literary components[20] that either point to even older traditions or are by now only figures of speech, as has happened with many mythical elements.[21] It is thus very difficult to point to parallels and distinguish between accidental and intentional ones.[22] It is nevertheless worth noting that even in recent years, theories are constantly proposed to identify vestiges or signs of the existence of Autumn Festivals. These indeed took place, if not in the Temple of Jerusalem (probably after the centralization of cult), then in the temples of the Northern Kingdom (particularly in Dan), which absorbed elements of the Canaanite cult. Later on, after the destruction of the Northern kingdom, these elements were incorporated into and assimilated by the Jerusalem ritual. It is possible that they were brought from the north by the Levites and were accepted, after

20. It stands to reason that even defining the Ark as "the Ark of God, which is called by the name of the Lord of hosts" (2 Sam. 6:2) points to a combination of ancient traditions. (I shall not go into the problem of the double word שם (SHEM).) Von Rad, *Theologie* (1958), vol. 1 p. 128; *Theology* (1962), vol. 1 pp. 122–123.
21. Seeligmann, "Cultic Tradition" (1964), argues that it was the ceremonial rites which created the myth, not the other way round.
22. In the dialogue between David and Michal, both speak of servants' maids. Michal says: "How the king of Israel honoured himself today, uncovering himself today before the eyes of his servants' maids, as one of the vulgar fellows shamelessly uncovers himself!" (2 Sam. 6:20), to which David replies: "I will make myself yet more contemptible than this, and I will be abased in your eyes; but by the maids of whom you have spoken, by them I shall be held in honour" (6:22). There is an interesting parallel in Ugarit, which is not sufficient to prove literary dependence. In the story of Baal it is told that when Baal rose to his feet and angrily leaves the banquet, he says: "Shall I drink at my table? Shall I drink my affront in my cup? Lo, two (kinds) of feasts does Baal hate, yea three the rider of the clouds [abhors]: a feast of shame, a feast of strife, and a feast about which maid-servants chatter; now shame comes forth in it, and maidservants chatter about it." (translation by Cassuto, "Baal" (1938/1975), p. 128.

some modification, in Jerusalem. In the course of this process of adaptation and assimilation, these symbols were fully accepted as idiomatic expressions.[23]

The current tendency is to reject theories of this nature as going too far.[24] Neverthless, they open up new avenues of interpretation.[25] What they all have in common is that they regard the events as an expression of David's respect for ancient symbols and traditions. This being so, the story naturally contains symbolic actions that were customary in these or similar circumstances, and whose roots probably predated the consolidation of the Israelite traditions.[26] In this connection it is less important to speculate whether these traditions are tribal with perhaps particular significance among the Northern Tribes.[27] What is important is the place of the sin in the story, and it seems to me that we must interpret the Uzzah episode differently.

23. For example, the mythological elements in certain hymns, and metaphors and combinations of phrases in the Psalms of Korah. Goulder, *Korah* (1982), points out that the main components of these psalms are of northern origin. For example: Psalms 42, 46, 47, 84, 87–89. As against this view, see the argument of Jeremias, *Königtum Gottes* (1987), esp. pp. 63–70.
24. See especially the critical comments of J.A. Galbraith, *CBQ* vol. 47 (1985), pp. 123–125.
25. One may also suppose that the story is structured on a pattern. Buber, *Moses* [E] (1946), pp. 60–63; *Moses* [G] (1948), pp. 72–74, pointed out four stages through which saviour-leaders must pass before they can undertake their task: fleeing, taking flocks to pasture, a vision test and a demonic encounter.
26. For example, David distributing gifts after the arrival of the Ark. Weinfeld, *Justice* (1985), p. 87, points out similar actions by Shalmaneser III.
27. Additional signs of a 'ritualistic' literature can be found here and there in the structure of 2 Sam. 6. Buber, *Königtum Gottes* (1932), p. 132 note 35 assumes that vss. 14–15 with the triple use of the words "and David" formed part of a poem: "ודוד מכרכר... ודוד חגור... ודוד וכל בית ישראל" [= "And David danced... and David was girded... So David and all the house of Israel..."]. But he sees the whole story as a realistic reflection of "innocent theocratic enthusiasm", which reaches its peak here.

Was it David who Sinned?

We should not conclude from the text that there was any intention, direct or indirect, of reprimanding David for erring or sinning. On the contrary, we may conclude that it was David who was doing the reprimanding; for had he recognized that his sins, or those of his men, had aroused the wrath of the Lord, we would have expected him to show signs of regret or beg for forgiveness. Not only is there no indication of any such attitude in the whole story, but it is the Ark that emits messages of reconciliation and appeasement. It is difficult to construe otherwise the bounties bestowed on the house of Obed-edom the Gittite[28] after the Ark was redirected there. This is also clear from the repetitions and the structure of the text in 2 Sam. 6:10–12.

	בית עבד אדם הגתי	ויטהו דוד
שלשה חדשים	בית עבד אדם הגתי	וישב ארון ה'
ואת כל ביתו	עבד אדם	ויברך ה' את
		ויגד למלך לאמר
ואת כל אשר לו	בית עבד אדם	ברך ה' את
בעבור ארון האלהים		
את ארון האלהים		וילך דוד ויעל
עיר דוד בשמחה	מבית עבד אדם	
(פס' 10–12)		

but David took it aside to the house of Obed-edom the Gittite

And the ark of the Lord remained in the house of Obed-edom the Gittite three months

and the Lord blessed Obed-edom and all his household

And it was told King David

28. As to the identity of Obed-edom the Gittite as one of David's veteran supporters, see McCarter, *II Samuel* (1984), p. 170.

The Lord has blessed the household of Obed-edom and all that belongs to him

because of the ark of God

So David went and brought up the ark of God

from the house of Obed-edom to the city of David with rejoicing

The events that occurred in the house of Obed-edom the Gittite can be interpreted as a victory won by David. Moreover, the feeling that it is David who is doing the reprimanding also comes from the description of his initial reaction: "And David was angry because the Lord had broken forth upon Uzzah" (2 Sam. 6:8); and "So David was not willing to take the ark of the Lord into the city of David; but David took it aside..." (2 Sam. 6:10). These expressions suggest that the initiative and the decision were David's. Therefore it is possible that the phrase "and David was afraid" (2 Sam. 6:9) does not deal merely with fear, but also with practical concern about carrying out the mission, which now seems impossible: "How can the ark of the Lord come to me?" (2 Sam. 6:9).[29]

Thus all the indications are that the text is emphasizing David's initiative and his control of the situation.[30] The increasing pace of the text, i.e., the gradual expansion of the details of the narrative from the moment the Ark was diverted to the house of Obed-edom

29. 'How' implying 'how is it possible' or 'why', indicating that it is really impossible, see Gen. 26:9; 39:9; Ex. 6:12, 30; 2 Sam. 2:22; 12:18 etc. Indeed the translation of this vs. in the JPS is: "How can I let the ark of the Lord come to me?" (2 Sam. 6:9); cf. NEB: "How can I harbour the Ark of the Lord after this?" and JB: "However can the Ark of Yahweh come to me?"
30. The parallel passage in Chronicles is "And David was afraid of God that day" (1 Chron. 13:12), but the addition of the words "of God" give that fear a less concrete character. (Cf. Gen. 20:11; Deut. 25:18). The Chronicler emphasizes David's initiative by replacing "how can the Ark of the Lord come...?" (2 Sam. 6:9) by "How can I bring...?" (1 Chron. 13:12).

the Gittite, serves to emphasize the festive nature of the occasion and makes untenable the assumption that the Uzzah incident had given rise solely to feelings of guilt or remorse. It is therefore also worthy of note that the cause of the Lord's anger (Uzzah's placing his hand on the Ark) is not understood as going counter to the joy engendered by bringing up the Ark.[31] The incident seems to be in keeping with all the other actions, as if Uzzah's putting out his hand was a perfectly natural thing to do, because they were coming to Nacon's threshing floor "making merry... with all their might, with songs[32] and lyres and harps and tambourines" (2 Sam. 6:5).

In the description the only thing that is out of place is the apparently unreasonable outburst of the Lord's wrath, and it seems to me most reasonable to regard this as having no cause or explanation. Like other outbursts of wrath or other manifestations of "the dark side of the Deity",[33] here too we have a manifestation of God's demonic aspect. However, this is not the main point of the text, which is rather David's reaction. From it we learn not only that David turned "the Lord's wrath into blessing",[34] but that he was bringing the Ark up to Jerusalem after it had been 'cleansed' and could no longer do any harm.[35] The symbolism of bringing the

31. Rashi states in his commentary: "'Stumbles' is an intransitive verb; their limbs failed them because of the holiness of the Ark." Nevertheless the rest of his exegesis returns to the sin: "It was not proper for it to be borne in a cart...".
32. It seems to me that we should read, as in the LXX, "with all their might, with song...", or as in 1 Chr. 13:8. But Ehrlich, *Mikra ki-Pheschuto* (1900), suggests to read בכלי (with instruments) instead of בכל (with all).
33. See Volz, *Das Dämonische* (1924). For more on his approach, see note 37 below. Similarly Eichrodt, *Theologie* (1948), vol. 1 p. 126; vol. 2 pp. 119–120; *Theology* vol. 1 (1961) p. 265; vol. 2 p. 227. For a general survey of the subject see Dunston, The Dark Side (1983). His conclusion is similar to that of Eichrodt, in that the biblical religion sees no contradiction between this facet of the Deity and His being a moral entity: the Deity who rules over all phases of life should also posses all conceivable qualities.
34. Kaufmann, *Religion* (1947), p. 169.
35. Baqon, "David" (1965), deals with the change that was introduced after the death of Uzzah, which enabled the Ark to be brought up to Jerusalem without

Ark up to Jerusalem is complex.[36] Clearly the story tells us not only that David promises the continued sanctification of ancient traditions by adopting their symbols, but also that adopting these symbols marks a turning-point, since he uproots from them elements that he regards as undesirable.[37] As I have indicated above in the Introduction, what we see here is a substansive change in the perception of the Deity. The historiographer apparently wishes to ascribe something like a revolution to David and his work, namely, an attempt to establish belief in a Deity who can no longer be

mishap. He believes we can learn from the Chronicler's text that after the Uzzah incident it was made sure the Ark would be carried only by Levites, "who were carrying the Ark of the covenant of the Lord" (1 Chr. 15:26). He believes that the Chronicler's is the right text, whereas the text in Samuel reflects a tendentious correction, since the original list in 1 Chr. was anti-Priest and pro-Levite. For more on this subject, see Grintz, "David" (1969).
Note that Noth, *Studien* (1943), passim; *D History* (1981), pp. 89–99, argues that "the Ark of the covenant" is basically a Deuteronomistic term.

36. I cannot deal here with the functions of the Ark after it was brought up to Jerusalem, and certainly not after the construction of the Temple. Fretheim, "Ark" (1968) thinks it fulfilled ritual functions until the reform of Josiah.
On the Ark as a symbol of the House of David, mainly on the basis of Psalm 132, see Maier, *Ladeheiligtum* (1965).

37. Jeremias, "Lade" (1971), points to Jer. 3:16 as evidence that the Ark tradition was displaced by the Jerusalem tradition, which, he thinks, is of much earlier origin. In his opinion, the change in the conception of the Ark can also be seen in the fact that, from the time the Ark is brought to Jerusalem, no more harmful acts are attributed to it, as in the Uzzah, Dagon or Beth-shemesh episodes.
But it is worth noting that Volz, *Das Dämonische* (1924), believes that there is a demonic element in the Deity, not only in the earliest stages of Israelite history. He notes several stages of development towards the refinement, or strengthening, of the spiritual side of the deity at the expense of the violent side. Whereas belief in the Lord of the Mountain (the Mountain of the Lord) is filled with fear and danger, the Exodus raised religion to a higher level: the Lord absorbed all the demonic elements and became the sole demon, stronger than all his predecessors. With the permanent settlement in the Land, His spiritual dimensions were emphasized more strongly, while the demonic elements were ascribed to other forces, mainly God's messengers, such as spirits, angels, and finally Satan.

regarded as capricious, ill-tempered, wrathful.[38] I shall be dealing with other aspects of this revolution later,[39] but if we wish to understand the message of the story, we must analyze this chapter (2 Sam. 6), in particular the ties between its two central episodes.

The Relationship of the Episodes of Uzzah and Michal

From the ideological point of view, the connection between the two episodes seems to be one of contrast: David, who succesfully brings a blessing upon the whole people, is not granted a blessing when it comes to his own house. Quite the contrary: he is cursed, in the full sense of the word.[40] The text stresses that this attitude towards him does not stem from his house, but from one who is presented as the representative of the House of Saul. Note the double emphasis on "Michal the daughter of Saul" in vss. 20 and 23, and also David's words: "[God] who chose me above your father and above all his house" (2 Sam. 6:21). This ideological conflict is not necessarily proof of the fundamental unity of the story. The

38. Eichrodt, *Theologie* (1948) vol. 1 pp. 230–231; *Theology* (1961), vol. 1 pp. 453 maintains that one of the most significant changes brought about by the kingdom was a shift in the emphasis in God's activities from nature to history. However, he does not ascribe the moderation or restraint in the demonic aspect of God to the kingdom. Generally speaking, Eichrodt fails to understand why the expressions of divine wrath are interpreted as characterizing an impulsive and capricious Deity: In his opinion, such acts as the plague that followed the census (2 Sam. 24) show that the Lord has certain demonic powers, but this still does not make Him a demon (see *Theology* p. 262).
39. As to further projections of the newly established kingdom on religious life, see Malamat, "Statecraft" (1970). He argues that since the historiographer mentions the Elders only in connection with the ritual of bringing the Ark into the Temple (1 Kings 8:1,3), he may have intended to ascribe a religious dimension to the kingdom, although there is no reason to doubt the function of the Elders as a political assembly.
40. The root קל"ה is used in the same sense in Genesis 16:4 ותקל גברתה בעיניה (she looked with contempt on her mistress). In particular see Weinfeld, "Curse" (1976); Cassuto, "Blessing" (1954); Eitrem, "Curses" (1970); Blank, "Curse" (1950); Brichto, *Curse* (1968).

Bible contains examples of complex stories, which are regarded as the result of the combining of two separate narratives, the very combination providing an additional and profound ideological dimension.[41] As we look more closely at some details of the structure, we notice that even if the story originally consisted of two separate ones, the combination was done with such artistry that division is difficult, almost impossible.

1. A *Leitwort* that appears throughout the chapter is על"ה (to go up or to bring up), in its various forms (vss. 2, 12, 15, 17, 18; to which we should perhaps add the preposition על (on), which appears in vss. 2. 7, 8, 10, 21).

2. A key phrase for both episodes is בר"ך (to bless), vss. 11, 12, 18, 20 generally appearing alongside בית (house), in vss. 3, 4, 5, 10, 11, 12, 15, 19, 20, 21. There may also be a connection between the motif ברך בית (bless the house) and the unusual phrase בית ישראל (house of Israel) which appears here twice, in vss. 5 and 15.[42] This may be intended to stress the blessing brought by David, particularly in contrast to the house of Saul, hinted at in the phrase "above your father and above all his house" (2 Sam. 6:21).

3. In the central sections of each of the two episodes the original Hebrew text indicates a poetic structure, i.e., a strophic one: identical beginnings, combinations of similar words, and to some extent metre.

41. See Uffenheimer, "Genesis 18–19" (1975).

42. The expression בית ישראל (= the house of Israel) is rather rare in the historiographic books, and most common in the book of Ezekiel, where it appears about 60 times. In the books of Samuel, it appears only three times (1 Sam. 7:3; 2 Sam. 1:12, 16:3). It also appears in Joshua 21:43 (MT) and 1 Kings 12:21. In all these instances it reflects national solidarity.

Vss. 2–4:

להעלות ... הכרבים ... עליו   וירכבו (alliteration)   אל עגלה חדשה
וישאוהו...   אשר בגבעה
נהגים...   העגלה חדשה
וישאהו...   אשר בגבעה

who sits enthroned on the cherubim. And they carried...

upon a new cart

and brought it out... which was on the hill

were driving the new cart

Vss. 10–12:

...בית עבד אדם הגתי
בית עבד אדם הגתי
ויברך ה׳ את   עבד אדם   ואת כל ביתו
ברך ה׳ את   בית עבד אדם
וילך... ויעל...   מבית עבד אדם

the house of Obed-edom the Gittite

the house of Obed-edom the Gittite

and the Lord blessed Obed-edom and all his household

the Lord has blessed the household of Obed-edom

went and brought up... from the house of Obed-edom

Vss. 14–15:

ודוד מכרכר בכל עז לפני ה׳
ודוד חגור אפוד בד
ודוד וכל בית ישראל מעלים את ארון ה׳

And David danced before the Lord with all his might;

and David was girded with a linen ephod

So David and all the house of Israel brought up the ark of the Lord

Vss. 17–18:

ויבאו... ויצגו... ויעל דוד עלות...
ויכל דוד מהעלות העולה... ויברך...

And they brought... and set it in its place... and David offered burnt offerings...

And when David had finished offering the burnt offerings... he blessed the people...

Vss. 20–21:

[מיכל:]

מה **נכבד** היום
מלך ישראל

אשר **נגלה** היום

לעיני אמהות עבדיו

כהגלות נגלות אחד
הרקים

[דוד:]

ונקלתי עוד מזאת
והייתי שפל **בעיני**
ועם **האמהות** אשר
אמרת
עמם **אכבדה**

[Michal:] How the king of Israel **honoured** himself today

uncovering himself today

before the **eyes of his servants' maids**

as one of the vulgar fellows shamelessly **uncovers** himself

[David:] I will make myself yet more contemptible than this
and I will be abased **in my eyes**

but by **the maids** of whom you have spoken

by them I shall be **held in honour**

4. The chapter is replete with verbs indicating movement, and the pictures they paint suggest augmentation and intensification of the festive movement, until it reaches its climax in "leaping and dancing" (2 Sam. 6:16).

5. Obviously, therefore, against this background of intensified movement, its cessation (or interruption) in both episodes is conspicuous; in the first, it is expressed by "stumbled" (vs. 6); and in the second by "looked out of the window" (vs. 16). Tension reaches its height in the contrast between "make contemptible" and "held in honour" (vs. 22).[43]

From these details one gets the general impression of a uniform structure, and it is therefore difficult to point to either of the two episodes as an appendage of secondary importance.[44]

Taken together, the two episodes contribute to the forming of David's image. The impression obtained is that David who forced the Ark to bring a blessing, was not himself exalted thereby. His spontaneous outbreak of joy is over the actual arrival of the Ark, and he belittles himself in deference to it. But, as has been said, in his own house this is misunderstood. There they declare that the king's honour takes precedence over respect for his deeds, and

43. This contrast serves as an argument against the LXX version: καὶ ἀποκαλυφθήσομαι (reflecting: ונגלתי?), as in vs. 20.

44. Schulte, *Geschichtsschreibung* (1972) pp. 144–145, thinks this is especially so with regard to the Michal episode.

perhaps even over the honour due to the Ark itself. The bitter irony in these words acquires added force if we recall that this is the first time David is addressed by anyone as "King of Israel".

This may be a rhetorical innuendo, contrasting the House of Saul and the House of David by means of their personal stories. Not only does David, who is capable of bringing a blessing upon his people, fail to bring one upon his own house; we might also interpret it to mean that the well-being of his house was sacrificed to his faith and devotion to the affairs of the kingdom.[45]

But since this lack of understanding is manifested by the representative of the House of Saul, it gives the author an additional opportunity to present the contrast between the two houses, with the House of Saul again appearing in a negative light. In fact, this is one of the characteristics of the description of David's rise to the throne and his initial actions. The author takes advantage of every opportunity to cast aspersions on the House of Saul, by means of juxtaposed antithetical analogies, such as the very act of bringing up the Ark — something which Saul neglected to do throughout his reign.[46]

These analogies hint at the preference the Lord has promised David.[47] Likewise, there are numerous hints as well as explicit statements (as in 2 Sam. 3:37: "So all the people and all Israel

45. The story constitutes some sort of explanation of the problem that arose in 2 Sam 3:13–16, where Michal was presented as a tragic victim of political considerations.
46. Especially Weiser, *Glaube* (1931), pp. 100, 115, 134. In his opinion, by bringing up the Ark, David gave a religious-ritualistic background to national unity. See also Abramski, "Monarchy" (1974), who believes that the main purpose of the story was to point out the superiority to the House of David over Saul, who throughout his reign, neglected the Ark.
47. Note the words of Abigail (1 Sam. 25:30), Abner (2 Sam. 3:9–10). Jonathan (1 Sam. 23:17; 20:15) and even Saul (1 Sam. 24:20). Perhaps this is also the intention of the words "all the tribes of Israel" in 2 Sam. 5:2.

understood that day that it had not been the king's will to slay Abner the son of Ner") about David's complete innocence with regard to the fall of the House of Saul.[48] The references to promises made by the Lord obviously carry a theological message; i.e., that David was preferred over Saul because of his greater faith. On the other hand the lesson implicit in the analogies is basically a political one.[49]

It emerges, then, that the two tendencies, the theological and the political struggle with the House of Saul, are to a considerable extent interwoven. Therefore the possibility arises that, if the author finds it important to tie his theological aim to critical innuendos directed against the House of Saul, the composition may possibly go back to a period when the echoes of that struggle were still clearly heard.[50]

And yet the contemporaneous aspect of the message is not the most important part of the story. The pretext of the conflict over the Michal episode (centered on Michal's curse as opposed to David's blessing) also indicates that the holiness of the Ark and the expression of David's devotion to his faith by bringing it up to Jerusalem, are the focal points. Were it not for the context and the detailed form in which the story is fashioned, it would have been possible to assume that the Uzzah incident was designed as a warning of the holiness of the Ark, and the great care with which it

48. I cannot accept the view that the literary unit 1 Sam. 15 — 2 Sam. 5 is nothing but an apologia for the House of David. In particular I cannot agree that David was actually involved in most of the acts recounted there, including the murder of Abner. See, for example Vanderkam, "Complicity" (1980); McCarter, "Apology" (1980).

49. There is a didactic emphasis in the words of David, which again present him as God's anointed (משיח ה'), and therefore inviolable: 1 Sam. 24:11 (MT); 26:9, 11; 2 Sam. 1:14, 16.

50. Campbell, "Ark" (1979), believes that the time of this narrative precedes the placing of the Ark in Solomon's Temple. Rost, *Thronnachfolge* (1926), pp.174; *Succession* (1981), p. 49, differs.

must be handled. Because of these details, however, it seems to me that one can state with certainty that the main point of the story is to show that it is David who is responsible for the blessing resulting from nullifying the Lord's wrath. In other words, David is bringing to Jerusalem a Deity who is no longer to be characterized as outbursting or wrathful.

It may be worth adding that, in contrast to the Deity's sudden explosion of wrath — which cannot be fully grasped or understood — David's actions are described in a way that indicates consideration and deliberation. One is left with the impression of careful planning of every detail, as expressed in vss. 1–4. The same careful, calculated planning also appears in vss. 9–12. The very detailed description of the joyful celebration (vss. 5, 13–15) contrasts sharply with the sudden, mysterious blow which is described so briefly in vs. 7 "and God smote him there", and the formula "and the anger of the Lord was kindled" (2 Sam. 6:7).

Thus the entire story is an array of contrasts. This adds weight to the theological message, which ascribes a change, perhaps a revolutionary one, in David's perception of the Deity. It is particularly significant that the book is so constructed that this is David's first important action immediately after the conquest of Jerusalem and his decisive victory over the Philistines (see above p. 33).[51] Similarly significant is the last act ascribed to David by the editors of the book: the story of the ending of the epidemic on the threshing floor of Araunah the Jebusite, which will be discussed in the next chapter.

51. There are some who maintain that 2 Sam. 6 represents the beginning of a new literary unit, whereas 2 Sam. 1–5 belong to the narrative that tells of the rise of David. e.g., Grønbaek, *Aufstieg* (1971), pp. 11–36 with bibliography; Flanagan, Traditions (1970), pp. 1–6.

CHAPTER TWO

THE CENSUS AND STOPPING THE PESTILENCE: 2 Sam. 24

The story of the census and the pestilence is another example of David's success in moderating an outburst of Divine rage. It is customary to consider chapter 24 as a chain of related events: the Lord became angry with the people of Israel (for a reason that is not clear) and incited David to carry out a census in Israel and Judah. David has the census taken, disregarding Joab's warnings of its grave consequences. Indeed, punishment came in the form of a pestilence, which David succeeded in bringing to halt on Araunah's threshing floor. David then bought the threshing floor, with the intention of building an altar there,[1] as instructed by the prophet Gad. The details are different in the Book of Chronicles — see pp. 60–64. But this sequence of events is not so simple, since the reason for its beginning is not apparent. The opening "Again the anger of the Lord was kindled against Israel" (vs. 1) raises two questions:

First, we do not know what had angered the Lord. The attempt to link this with the story of Saul, the Gibeonites and the famine described in 2 Sam. 21,[2] with the suggestion that the Lord was still

1. About the custom of building the sanctuary on the king's land, see von Rad, *Theologie* vol. 1 (1958), p. 51; *Theology* vol. 1 (1962), pp. 42–43. See also Galling, "Stifter" (1950) ; Johnson, *Kingship* (1955), p. 47.
2. Thus Levi ben Gershom (רלב"ג). See also Thenius, *Bücher Samuels* (1842), p. 255; Bleek, *Einleitung* (1878), p. 232; Budde, *Samuelbücher* (1902), pp. 305–306, 326–327; *Samuel* (1894), pp. 84–86. In the latter's opinion there is no clear reason for the Lord's wrath. See Hertzberg, *Samuelbücher* (1960), pp. 337–342;

angry over the sins of Saul and his house for killing the Gibeonites, does not have sufficient basis. Rashi (and following him Kimhi) simply says: "I do not know why".[3]

Secondly, it is not self-evident that the census is to be viewed as a sin. The necessity to take precautions over it, implies that it might involve a danger,[4] as we learn from other sources, e.g., Ex. 30, in particular vs. 12: "then each shall give a ransom for himself to the Lord when you number them, that there be no plague among them when you number them." (See also Ex. 38:25–26, which deals in detail with "...the silver from those of the congregation who were numbered".[5] Something similar seems to have occurred with Saul, who before going out to do battle with the Amalekites, counted the people בטלאים (either at a place called Telaim, or by means of young goats), that is, he did not count them directly (1 Sam. 15:4).[6] But other parts of the Bible mention a census without any precautions (particularly when it is a divine command: "Take a census of all the congregation of the people of Israel", Num. 1:2); in those cases no precautionary measures are required, as if conducting a

Samuel (1964), pp. 408–415 and also McCarter, *II Samuel* (1984), p. 509, who adds that the connection with the story of the Gibeonites is the work of the redactor.

3. See the treatment of the subject by Abrabanel. He argues against Levi ben Gershom and Nahmanides, but he himself believes that the sin of Israel is the revolt of Sheba ben Bichri.
4. Eichrodt, *Theologie* (1948), vol. 1 p. 124; *Theology* (1961), vol. 1 p. 262 believes that this episode, like several others (Ex. 4:21; 9:12; Jud. 9:23; 1 Sam. 2:25), reveals the Deity as possessing certain demonic powers, but that this fact does not make the Lord a demon. See above Introduction, note 45.
5. Some think that this belief is common in the Bible. See Rofé, Angelology (1969), passim; cf. also note 6.
6. See Licht, *Numbers* (1985), p. 8. For a more detailed treatment of the subject, especially with regard to the connection between the census and the pestilence see McCarter, *II Samuel* (1984), p. 512. While rejecting the view that the episode shows signs of Mari's influence, where the census called for ritual cleansing as well. For surveys of this theme, see Bright, *History* (1972), pp. 201–203, 246; Cross, *Canaanite Myth* (1974), pp. 227–228, 240.

census was taken for granted (Josh. 8:10; Jud. 7:3; 1 Sam. 13:15; 2 Kings 3:6).[7] In each of these cases the census is required by a situation of war, and for purely military reasons; the accepted view is that every census serves that particular purpose.[8]

Licht thinks that there is danger in a census held simply for purposes of propaganda i.e., to display the strength of the kingdom.[9] The relation between such propaganda and political necessity is something this study has to deal with. The story about the census may reflect disapprobation not because the act itself is sinful, but for some other reason, probably political.[10]

The detailed description in vss. 5–7 hints that the purpose of the census was not military (as may be inferred from vs. 4: "But the king's word prevailed against Joab and the commanders of the army... went out from the presence of the king to number the people of Israel". At any rate, it is not exclusively military: "They crossed the Jordan, and encamped in Aroer, and from the city that

7. See Loewenstamm, "Census" (1968). From the phrase "valiant men who drew the sword" (2 Sam. 24:9), he concludes that the aim of David's census was military.
8. Licht, *Numbers* (1985), p. 8. He quotes from *Bereshit Rabba*, Chapter 2, end of paragraph 17: "Whenever Israel counted their number for a reason, they were not in want; but when they counted their number for no purpose, they were in want."
9. The artificiality of the figures is self-evident, since they are rounded to the hundreds of thousands. The ostentatious nature of the census is revealed not only by the exaggerated figures (see M. Broshi, "The Expansion of Jerusalem in the Reigns of Hezekiah and Manasseh", *IEJ* vol. 24 (1974), pp. 21–26; Y. Shiloh, "The Population of Iron Age Palestine in the Light of Urban Plans, Areas and Population Density", *EI* vol. 15 (1981), pp. 274–282 [Hebrew]), but also by the disproportion between Judah and Israel, which was certainly meant to enhance the prestige of Judah.
10. The story is very old, possibly dating from the time of David himself. See von Rad, *Theologie* (1958), vol. 1 p. 316; *Theology* (1962), vol. 1 p. 317, who claims that the story of the census is incomparably older than the story of the succession to the throne.

is in the middle of the valley, toward Gad and on to Jazer. Then they came to Gilead, and to the land of Tahtim-hodshi, and they came to Dan-jaan and they went around to Sidon, and came to the fortress of Tyre and to all the cities of the Hivites and Canaanites; and they went out to the Negeb of Judah at Beer-sheba" (vss. 5–7 MT). Nor is there mention of any military operation which may justify the statement "In Israel there were eight hundred thousand valiant men who drew the sword, and the men of Judah were five hundred thousand" (vs. 9). Specifying areas that indicate territorial expansion[11] may mean that the census served to establish extended political control. It stands to reason that it also had something to do with the orderly collection of taxes,[12] especially in territories that did not consider themselves under David's sovereignity and administration.[13]

The author of Chronicles is apparetnly unfamiliar with the frontiers of David's domain before they were extended. He sees no need to specify the new areas, and indeed makes no mention of them. Likewise, in his version of Joab's words (1 Chr. 21:3 as opposed to 2 Sam. 24:3) he tries to explain to David that the very holding of a census is a sin.

It becomes clear from the story that the census aroused some opposition which is represented by the Lord's anger and the pestilence. It contains an echo of the tension and anxiety over

11. Von Rad, *Theologie* (1958), vol. 1 p. 68; *Theology* (1962), vol. 1 p. 59; "Day of Yahweh" (1959) too, thinks that the purpose of the census was military, and he stresses that the story of the census and the pestilence (2 Sam. 24) contains an element of opposition to this step, since it conflicts with the traditional Holy War concepts. Also see Kallai, *Historical Geography* (1986), pp. 37–40. On the purpose of this, as of any census see Na'aman, *Borders* (1986), 98–102.
12. Mendenhall, "Political Society" (1960); Bendor, *BET-AB* (1986), passim.
13. A similar opinion is held by McCarter, *II Samuel* (1984), p. 509, based on the work of Herrmann, *Geschichte* (1973), pp. 202–203; *History* (1975), p. 157. Alt, "Königtum" (1951); "Monarchy" (1968), believes that the purpose of the census was to give official justification to the annexation of territory, in particular as detailed in verse 7.

David's decision to flaunt his military and political power. It may be, then, that the detailed enumeration of the regions gives a hint of the reason for the opposition to the entire census. The words of Joab, who in other instances too shows a realistic political sense (even when it becomes clear that he does not fully grasp David's intention or really understand his objectives[14]) also reflect awareness of the tension. In addition, the fact that Joab and "the commanders of the army" (2 Sam. 24:4) are charged with executing the task may strengthen the assumption that the census had an ulterior motive, and therefore aroused opposition in the upper circles of the North.[15] Interestingly enough, 1 Chr. 21 speaks of שרי העם "the commanders of the people" rather than שרי החיל in 2 Sam. 24:4, since it seems clear that שרי החיל "the commanders of the army" is a purely military term. Likewise, Chronicles adds in vs. 6: "But he did not include Levi and Benjamin in the numbering, for the king's command was abhorrent to Joab." The comment is not entirely clear, though it is possible that the author of Chronicles ascribes to Joab an intention to avoid deprecating Benjamin and Levi, who were particularly sensitive about their status in the Kingdom of David.[16]

Excursus
Contradictions and Tensions in the Story in 2 Sam. 24 and in 1 Chr. 21

1. In 2 Sam. 24 there is a contradiction between vs. 16 and what follows. Even though it says in vs. 16 "the Lord repented of the evil,

14. The disparity between David's attitude and that of Joab becomes very evident in the matter of the assassination of Abner. See above Introduction note 57. Cf. also Hempel, *Geschichten* (1964), pp. 30 ff.
15. The very imposition of the tax was interpreted as a blow to tribal society and its mode of life. Reviv, *Clan* (1979), pp. 119–134 believes that in 2 Sam. 24, the hostile attitude towards the census is preserved, an attitude characteristic of a tribal society and a population unaccustomed to a centralized regime.
16. See Japhet, *Chronicles H* (1977), pp. 234–235, 398; *Chronicles ET* (1989), pp. 275, 473–474, who explains why this story has been included in Chronicles.

and said to the angel who was working destruction among the people 'It is enough; now stay your hand'", vs. 17 goes on to say: "Then David spoke to the Lord when he saw the angel who was smiting the people, and said, 'Lo, I have sinned, and I have done wickedly; but these sheep, what have they done?...". Thus it appears that the angel continues to smite the people of Israel. Even in vss. 21 and 25 the pestilence continues, for David explains to Araunah the reason for coming to see him: "To buy the threshing floor from you, in order to build an altar to the Lord, that the plague may be averted from the people..." (vs. 21); only later do we read: "So the Lord heeded supplications for the land, and the plague was averted from Israel" (vs. 25). In my opinion, the editor-author may have rearranged (disarranged?) the order of events on purpose, to emphasize David's initiative and his part in terminating the pestilence. To that end he moved David's words from their original place, so that the final and most impressive chord should not express the Lord's regret, but rather His response to David's entreaty.

2. It is clear from vss. 18–19 that David went up to Araunah's threshing floor by order of the Lord, passed on by Gad. But according to vs. 17 David was already there, and had met the angel.[17] As the story is told in the Book of Chronicles, David met the angel on Araunah's threshing floor and it was only later that the angel ordered him, through Gad, to return and build an altar there (1 Chr. 21:18).

* * *

This reflects tension, mainly political, transferred to the theological level.

To clarify the intention of the story we must compare additional details with the Chronicler's version.

17. Rofé, Angelology (1969).

The first difference, one that has been widely dealt with, comes at the very beginning of the story. Instead of 2 Sam. 24:1: "Again the anger of the Lord was kindled against Israel" the Chronicler's text reads: "Satan stood up against Israel, and incited David..." (1 Chr. 21:1). The Chronicler, in accordance with his outlook, cannot possibly attribute to the Lord an intention (which is not even clearly rationalized), to make David fail. So he attributes it to Satan.[18] In this way he dispenses with the Lord's wrath against Israel. But the difference in the texts also highlights the fact that the author of the Book of Samuel did not hesitate to describe God's inexplicable manifestations of anger towards Israel, and saw no difficulty whatsoever in this. The comparison shows not only the different conception that had evolved during the time that elapsed between the writing of the Book of Samuel and that of Chronicles, but also that the author of Samuel is still close to a concept that tolerates the existence of a violent, wrathful Deity. This accords with what we saw in the story of Uzzah.

The second difference is also connected with the fact that the author of the Book of Samuel was closer than the Chronicler to the events he describes. The latter places the purchase of the threshing floor close not only to the construction of the altar, but also to David's declaration "Here shall be the house of the Lord" (1 Chr. 22:1),[19] which is followed immediately by a description of the practical steps he took to prepare for building the Temple (vss. 2–19). This description accords with the Chronicler's general

18. Japhet, *Chronicles H* (1977), p. 129 and note 429; *Chronicles ET* (1989), p. 146 and note 427.

19. This declaration follows a detailed explanation that the tabernacle and the sacrificial altar were at that time in Gibeon. "For the tabernacle of the Lord, which Moses had made in the wilderness, and the altar of burnt offering were at that time in the high place at Gibeon, but David could not go before it to inquire of God, for he was terrified of the sword of the angel of the Lord." (1 Chr. 21:29–30). These words contain a kind of belated justification for removing the altar from Gibeon. For the role of Gibeon, see 1 Kings 3:5; 9:2 etc. See also Rofé, Angelology, (1969).

tendency to magnify David's part in building the Temple (even at the expense of Solomon).[20] Had these details been accurate they would certainly have suited the purpose of the author of the Book of Samuel, who would not have hesitated to include them. But he could not credit David with Solomon's actions, as the author of Chronicles could, because, at the time the book of Samuel was written, the details of David's and Solomon's lives were still widely known.[21]

The third discrepancy is conspicuous in the presentation of the events preceding the termination of the pestilence. The story as told in the Book of Samuel, is a continuous chain of events: David builds the altar, brings peace offerings and burnt offerings as sacrifices to the Lord, and the Lord is placated and the plague ceases (vs. 25). This sequence of events makes the Lord's action appear to be a direct response to the sacrifices, and this could seem almost magical. For that reason the author of Chronicles, breaks the direct tie with the words "and the plague was averted from Israel" (2 Sam. 24:25), by inserting "and he answered him with fire from heaven upon the altar of burnt offerings" (1 Chr. 21:26); cf. 1 Kings 18:37–38.[22]

A fourth difference lies in the presentation of the relationship between punishment and repentance. In the Book of Samuel David's penitence seems to be self-generated. Right after the report on the result of the census (vs. 9) the text reads: "But David's heart smote him after he had [MT: אחרי כן[23]] numbered the people", and David immediately expresses his repentance.[24] This

20. Japhet, *Chronicles H* (1977), pp. 393–401; *Chronicles ET* (1989), pp. 467–478.
21. Mosis, *Untersuchungen* (1973), p. 218 points out that the aetiological emphasis in the story as told in Chronicles is on finding a place for the Temple.
22. On God's response by fire, see Newsome, "New Understanding" (1975), p. 203.
23. Kimhi interprets אחרי כן to mean "after which", even though in most MSS of the Septuagint there is no כן. It seems to me that MT is preferable.
24. Most modern commentators think that vs. 10 is superfluous, and is a later

being so the Divine retaliation is already a certain mitigation of the punishment, and yet the blow itself is difficult to understand. One might suggest that once the Lord has been made angry it is impossible to annul the result of His wrath completely, and He leaves the choice of punishment to David. But the choice only emphasizes the extent to which David has become a tragic 'partner' in the decision.[25] In Chronicles however, the order is changed: "But God was displeased with this thing and he smote Israel" (vs. 7), and as a result of this change David expresses repentance which has an external cause "And David said to God: 'I have sinned greatly in that I have done this thing...'" (vs. 8).

That the Chronicler's version is deliberately different from that of Samuel is also clear from the fact that the former does not specify what is meant by "and he smote Israel" (1 Chr. 21:7), i.e., how the Lord struck to bring about David's repentance. The reason for this is that he cannot possibly invent another disaster. Thus it is clear that he has changed the text (as he has a habit of doing) to make it conform to his *Weltanschaung,* while remaining as faithful as possible to the language of his source.[26]

In this, too, we can see that the outburst of the wrath of God is not altogether alien to the author of the book of Samuel, although it goes counter to his general outlook. In any case, it does not embarrass him as much as it seems to embarrass the Chronicler, because the intention of the author of Samuel is to place on record the circumstances in which this change of faith took place.

addition. But comparison with the order in 1 Chr. 21 confirms the claim that the verse is in its proper place.

25. Rofé, Angelology (1969) believes that the story itself reflects the weakening of the tension normally existing between the older ritual, which contains some degree of exorcistic magic, and the element of the sovereignty of the Lord's will, as He himself announces the proper ritual is at the appropriate time.
26. On this practice in Chronicles see Rudolph, *Chronikbücher* (1955); Willi, *Auslegung* (1972); Japhet, *Chronicles H* (1977); *Chronicles ET* (1989).

The common factor in the differences tends to support the conclusion concerning the purpose of the story. The context in Chronicles stresses the aetiological aspect of the story in choosing the site for the temple,[27] whereas in the Book of Samuel the essence of the story is David's arresting of the Lord's anger. The writer of the 2 Sam. 24 is not disturbed by presenting the Lord as provoking David in an outburst of inexplicable wrath. Nor does he hesitate to describe the Lord's immediate response to the sacrifices in a way that looks almost like mechanical magic. The representation of the punishment following David's repentance as incomprehensible, and perhaps even from a theological and moral point of view superfluous, — is not alien to the religious beliefs presented in the book of Samuel. Its object is to present David as the agent of change. The altar he builds, on the site he bought because the pestilence was arrested there, is meant to commemorate the cessation of God's wrath.

As to the Divine wrath itself, it may perhaps be explained as reflecting the prevailing opposition to David's demonstrative action of carrying out the census, which his opponents regarded as an exhibitionist method of asserting his dominance.[28] In a way the Divine wrath may reflect the general tension, or the internal crisis caused by the changes in the traditional framework. The organization of the state by the monarchy must have given rise to apprehension and anxiety. In the story of the census attention is diverted from the political to the theological level. This is apparent more in the solution the author offers than in the conflict: while the anxiety over the impending changes is symbolized by God's wrath, the solution is symbolized by David's action.[29] In the story of bringing the Ark up to Jerusalem, as in the census and the stopping of the

27. On the data connected with temples and on the purchase of the Araunah threshing floor, Mt. Moriah, etc. See Haran, "Temples" (1978).

28. Japhet, *Chronicles H* (1977), pp. 234–235; *Chronicles ET* (1989), pp. 275–276.

29. Von Rad, *Theologie* vol. 1 (1958), p. 316 maintains that within the framework of the story as the *hieros logos* of Jerusalem, the place symbolizes the action of

pestilence on Araunah's threshing floor, there is an implied promise that the changes will all be for the good.[30] In this chapter, the change is expressed mainly by the purchase of the threshing floor as a site for an altar to the Lord. It stands to reason that commemorating the act of arresting the Divine wrath also serves to perpetuate the memory of David as a man who knew how to deal with a catastrophy.

To grasp more fully the nature of the changes we must clarify other incidents, in particular the prophecy of Nathan — 2 Sam. 7.

It is clear, however, that both instances, the Uzzah incident and the stopping of the pestilence, imply protests against the Divine outbursts of wrath. In the story of bringing up the Ark, the protest is expressed in David's initial reaction in refusing to go on to Jerusalem with it. In the story of the end of the pestilence, David is certainly making a protest when he says: "Lo I have sinned, and I have done wickedly; but these sheep, what have they done?" (2 Sam. 24:17).[31] This is similar to criticisms of the Lord in other parts of the Bible, e.g., in the Korah affair, when Moses says: "...shall one man sin, and wilt thou be angry with all the congregation?" (Num. 16:22).[32] Indeed, in both the Uzzah affair and the story of the pestilence, the protests lead to change. In the story of the Ark blessings are bestowed on the house of Obed-edom and in the second story David is commanded to construct an altar on the Araunah threshing floor in order to stop the pestilence (2 Sam.

David, in placing himself completely at the mercy of the Ark and its symbolic nature.

30. For theories on the functions of the Ark and its symbolic nature, see Chapter One notes 11 & 15.

31. Note that in the text of Chronicles, the element of protest comes out even more strongly, because of the emphasis (1 Chr. 21:17: "Was it not I who gave command to number the people? It is I who have sinned..." and the ending: "but let not the plague be upon thy people."

32. The composition of Num. 16 is not clear, see Noth, *Numeri* (1966), pp. 107–114; *Numbers* (1980), pp. 118–131; Liver, "Korah" (1961).

24:18, 21).[33] It is therefore reasonable to suppose that God's outbursts and his manifestations of himself as a god of wrath, are contrary to David's *Weltanschauung*. The steps he takes to institutionalize religion — i.e., placing the Ark in the capital and planning a permanent abode for the deity — indicate the direction of his new conception, which is the very opposite of the temporal and the arbitrary.

At the same time it should be pointed out that collective punsihment for the sin of an individual, especially the sin of the king, is not only a recurrent phenomenon in the Bible,[34] but is also within David's own experience. In 2 Sam. 21 the famine that the country suffered is explained as a punishment for the sins of Saul and his House against the Gibeonites.[35] But David, who in 2 Sam. 24 shows himself quite capable of protesting "but these sheep what have they done?" (vs. 17), does not do so when the cause of trouble is the House of Saul. Hence, from a comparison of the cases, it emerges that when the reference is to the House of Saul, the Lord's wrath is ostensibly justified.

33. Note that the close contact of the building of the altar and the stopping of the pestilence appears only in David's words to Araunah in vs. 21: "To buy the threshing floor of you, in order to build an altar to the Lord, that the plague may be averted from the people", and not in God's command spoken by Gad. This, too, was meant to stress the importance of David's initiative.
34. See, for example, Micah 3:11–12. For a discussion on the relation between prophecy and monarchy see Eichrodt, *Theologie* (1948), vol. 1 pp. 230–232; *Theology* (1962), pp. 450–452; Schmidt, "Kritik" (1971).
35. Much is unclear in the story in 2 Sam. 21. According to Bartal, *Saul* (1982), however, it is unreasonable to suppose that Saul would dare deliberately to break the sanctified pact with the Gibeonites. It is probable that the Gibeonites gave Saul sufficient cause to accuse them of breaking the agreement, since they came to the assistance of the Philistines in their war against him. This approach is based on Auerbach, *Wüste* (1938), vol. 1 p. 220; Bright, *History* (1972), p. 180; Blenkinsopp, *Gibeon* (1972), p. 56.
2 Sam. 21:1: "אל שאול ואל בית הדמים" is rendered in the Septuagint as 'Επὶ Σαουλ καὶ ἐπὶ τὸν οἶκον αὐτοῦ. It seems that MT has come down to us in a somewhat garbled form. It should have read: אל שאול ואל ביתה דמים. See Wellhausen, *Samuel* (1871), pp. 208–209; Driver, *Notes* (1913), p. 349–350.

The juxtaposition of the two events again points to the convergence of politics and theology: the tendency to present David and his actions as responsible for a new departure in the realm of religion is closely allied with the inclination to condemn the House of Saul and represent it as rejected and punished by the Lord.[36] (Of course, all this would be even more obvious if there were a direct link between chapters 21 and 24).[37] Apparently, the close tie between political and theological trends indicates the degree to which the ideological struggle was historically relevant. Obviously, I have no way of knowing whether the barbs directed at the House of Saul were propaganda weapons employed at the time of the actual conflict, or were used, with the perspective of hindsight, to justify the policies and victory of the House of David.[38] It is also possible that the intention was to attack only what the House of Saul stood for from an ideological point of view (i.e., ideas and views current before the 'revolution' ascribed to David). The former possibility is beyond the scope of this study, and clearly I cannot simply reconstruct the historical events. As to the other possibilities, it is clear that one can best discover the negative characteristics of the House of Saul by setting it against what we are told about David and his actions. Except for the hints I have mentioned, and others which are similar, the text dealing with these events does not disclose what was reprehensible in the House of Saul.[39]

36. On the obvious intention to censure and belittle the house of Saul, see Luriah, *Benjamin* (1970).
37. Smith, *Samuel* (1899), p. 388; McCarter, *II Samuel* (1984), pp. 440–441.
38. Luriah, *Benjamin* (1970); McCarter, "Apology" (1980); Vanderkam, "Complicity" (1980).
39. The reasons given in 1 Samuel for the rupture between Saul and Samuel and the ensuing crisis are not relevant for the present study, since in the narratives before us David's advantageous position in comparison with Saul's does not stem from the difference in their obedience to the word of God.

CHAPTER THREE

2 Sam. 6 and 24:

COMPARISONS AND CONCLUSIONS

The two stories — bringing up the Ark (2 Sam. 6) and stopping the pestilence (2 Sam. 24) — reveal certain common elements:

(a) In both, the Lord strikes a death blow.

(b) The reason for the fatal blow is not clarified in either.[1]

(c) In both David's reaction contains an element of protest. In the story of the Ark, the protest is in his action, which makes it more drastic than in the story of the pestilence, where it takes the form of words only.

(d) Bringing up the Ark and the census, are both symbolic, demonstrative, even exhibitionist acts.[2] What David is doing in bringing up the Ark to Jerusalem is that he is adopting its meaning and traditions which he is about to transform into a symbol of his capital. Judging by the festivities surrounding the event — a central symbol. The census plays a similar role: even though basically any census is carried out for organizational purposes, (army recruitment or levying taxes), I incline to the view that in the present case its main purpose is to demonstrate political strength. This is because of the context, the definition of the act as sinful, and the places mentioned.[3]

1. See above, Introduction note 45 & Chapter Two note 4.
2. See above, Chapter One notes 13 & 14, and Chapter Two notes 11, 14 & 15.
3. See above Chapter Two notes 9 & 11. For recent discussion see Na'aman, *Borders* (1986), pp. 44–47.

(e) In both cases there is an interlocking of the religious and the political planes. Undoubtedly bringing up the Ark has political connotations,[4] while the census, since it leads to establishing an altar on Araunah's threshing floor, has religious connotations.

(f) Both stories contain either hints or explicit statements that stress the positive in David as against the negative in Saul and his House, despite the fact that these are unnecessary for the development of the plot. The explicit comment is made by David when he says to Michal: "It was before the Lord, who chose me above your father, and above all his house" (2 Sam. 6:21),[5] and even the concluding statement of the narrative: "And Michal the daughter of Saul had no child to the day of her death" (2 Sam. 6:23), is tendentious.[6] The innuendoes can be found in the antithetical analogies: David brings up the Ark as his first act after his victory over the Philistines, whereas Saul refrained from doing so throughout his entire reign; and in the second story, David protests against the collective punishment that was imposed because of the census, but not against the three years of famine caused by the sin of : "... bloodguilt on Saul and on his house" (2 Sam. 21:1).

From the point of view of both meaning and message the position of the two narratives is significant. Some scholars believe

4. The political purpose of bringing up the Ark becomes even clearer in the Chronicler's version. The list (1 Chron. 11:10–12:41), is intended to create the impression that men from all the tribes participated in bringing up the Ark. See Japhet, *Chronicles H* (1977), pp. 228–231, 334–335; *Chronicles ET* (1989), pp. 267–270, 395–396.
5. According to the Septuagint translation: "Before the Lord I will dance... ", and in LXX^{L}: "truly as the Lord lives." We must not exclude the possibility that Lucian reflects the original text.
6. 2 Sam. 6:23 could be intended to preclude any claims by pretended heirs of the House of Saul: Hempel, *Literatur* (1930), p. 108; cf. Luriah, *Benjamin* (1970). I myself am unable to deal with the contradiction between this and 2 Sam. 21:8: "... and the five sons of Merab the daughter of Saul, whom she bore to Adriel the son of Barzillai the Meholathite."

that 2 Sam. 5 concludes the story of David's ascent to the throne.[7] If that is so, the story of bringing up the Ark (2 Sam. 6) not only tells of David's first significant deed after throwing off the Philistine pressure, but is also a fresh beginning from the point of composition. But even if we do not consider 2 Sam. 6 as a new departure from the techincal standpoint, from the point of view of their significance the two stories clearly constitute a framework: these are David's first and last acts as king on the domestic front.[8] It is undoubtedly of major significance that the report of David's activities is within a sort of frame, with the first and last deeds designed to arrest the Lord's wrath.[9] Moreover, the deeds that diverted the Divine wrath were not accidental: they were new (or renewed) foundations for a cult.[10] There cannot be any doubt that such a step would be interpreted as a declaration of a new perception (which is symbolized in the renewed cult).[11] Innovations are always disturbing, especially in conservative circles, and even more to people with privileged positions based on earlier traditions.[12]

7. Flanagan, Traditions (1970), pp. 1–6; Grønbaek, *Aufstieg* (1971), pp. 11–36.
8. The intention behind the order of events is even more apparent in I Chronicles, according to which the Ark was brought up to Jerusalem immediately after the capture of the city. The description of the victory in the valley of Rephaim/Baal-perazim appears after the Uzzah incident (1 Chron. 13–14).
9. Eichrodt, *Theologie* (1948), vol. 1 pp. 230–231; *Theology* (1961), vol. 1 p. 453 notes that acts that are patently supernatural are an element of belief in God. Even when the Lord's will is expressed by creative acts and by the introduction of order and stability, e.g., when giving the Law, he makes his appearance through thunder and lightning, fire and smoke that no human being can withstand. As against this, one of the striking changes brought about by the establishment of the kingdom is the shift of the emphasis in God's deeds from nature to history. This, he maintains, ties in with the process of abandoning the charismatic concept of the kingdom.
10. There is no reason to doubt the accuracy of the tradition that identifies the place of the Temple with Araunah's threshing floor. Greenberg, "Religion" (1979).
11. See above Chapter One notes 13, 14, 15 and Chapter Two notes 11, 25, 29.
12. As to the status of the Elders, one must note what is written about Absalom's revolt, where the Elders of Israel are mentioned as the people closest to

From a literary point of view, the Lord's outbursts of wrath may be an expression of these anxieties.[13] We may assume that the stories are a response to apprehensions of this kind, setting people's minds at rest: admittedly the Lord was angry, but in the end anger turned into a blessing.[14] However another interpretation seems preferable to me, i.e., that both stories are a polemic against the very concept of the Lord's explosive wrath as one of His characteristics. It seems to me that placing the Ark in the kingdom's capital and laying the foundation for the building of the Temple[15] do not represent only a territorial concept, that is, a proclamation of the change of the Deity's location: the announcement of the fact that from now on, the Deity has an unchanging, permanent abode, may have been meant to make it clear that in the future the Deity must be associated with unchanging behaviour — the Lord is not capricious, nor is He given to unpredictable outbursts. He does not

Absalom (2 Sam. 17:4). It is thought possible that one of the reasons for the masses' joining in the revolt was Absalom's purported promise to restore the tribal institutions to their former status. It is reasonable to suppose that the concern of the Elders about their status is an example of people who feared that the changes resulting from the establishment of the monarchy might effect their own interests. McKenzie, "Elders" (1959); Tadmor, "Political Institutions" (1968); see also Malamat, "Statecraft" (1970), and the definition by Reviv, *Clan* (1979), pp. 152–154; *Elders* (1989), pp. 87–90, of "the men of Israel" and "the men of Judah" as class distinctions.

13. Otto, *Heilige* (1927); *Holy* (1969), believes that the early stage of belief, expressed by the fear of demons no longer prevailed in the days of the Prophets and the Psalmists, but does not say when the change was made and how it was accomplished. See also note 9 above. For a survey of the subject see also Dunston, The Dark Side (1983).
    As to the Lord's power to kill, which can be countered only through the death ritual as part of traditions about Moses, see Greenberg, *Exodus* (1969), pp. 110–113; cf. Frankfort, *Kingship* (1948), pp. 143–212; 277–312; Albright, *Gods of Canaan* (1968).
14. Kaufmann, *Religion* (1947), p. 163.
15. The difference between viewing the Temple as the seat of God (as in 2 Sam. 7:5–6 and 1 Kings 8:13) or as the place of His name, as in many Deuteronomistic expressions is not important at this stage. Cf. Mazar, "Kingship" (1973).

destory His own works in an inexplicable rage: on the contrary, his actions are predictable and unambiguous.[16]

The survey in the Introduction leads to the conclusion that in the North, there was widespread belief in a Deity whose ways are strange and beyond human understanding, and whose apostles, the 'men of God' often act in a similar fashion. (This may even have been typical of tribal tradition generally, which vested authority in the elders.[17]) German biblical research commonly maintains that in other spheres too, such as the organization of governmental power, tribal traditions were preserved in the Northern Kingdom, but not in Judah.[18] I am not sure if one can conclude from this that our stories are in the nature of an ideological-theological controversy of South versus North. In my opinion, it is more correct to see them as justifying the new against the old,[19] and primarily as extolling David's enterprise in initiating a new departure, indeed a

16. For a discussion about the remote and hidden Deity in the ancient Near East and in the Old Testament, see Balentine, *Hidden God* (1983).
17. This is more or less the approach of Eichrodt, *Theologie* (1948), vol. 1 pp. 6–24; *Theology* (1961), vol. 1 pp. 36–69; except that he believes that this attitude towards the Deity, including a feeling of remoteness, is the result of a withdrawal from the relationship of covenant that became evident in the Northern Kingdom under the influence of the Canaanites' attitude towards their deity. See also his comments on the changes following the establishment of the monarchy, especially after the Ark was moved to Jerusalem.
18. Alt, "Königtum" (1951); "Monarchy" (1968); Noth, "Gott, König, Volk" (1950); "God, King and Nation" (1966); and as against that, Ishida, "Solomon's Succession" (1982).
19. Von Rad, *Theologie* (1958), vol. 1 pp. 56–65; *Theology* (1962), vol. 1 pp. 48–56, thinks that the change took place with the establishment of the monarchy in David's time. Among the changes was also a different concept of the activities of the Lord. From now on, His intervention in events is less apparent. This, he thinks, is the spirit expressed in the J stories such as Gen. 24, where the Lord responds to prayer, but no longer performs visible miracles. Here the author seems to prefer instruction of the heart to external experience. This view is not universally accepted. Rofé, "Rebekah" (1976), ascribes authorship of Gen. 24

revolution — from the theological point of view. This departure serves as a basis for a new faith upon which David's kingdom rests. It may well be that during the final stages of the drafting of the stories their editor-author regarded the House of Saul[20] as representing the old and its values. This could also be the reason for linking the critical comments and innuendos about the house of Saul with expressions of approbation for David's undertaking. This is a far-reaching hypothesis, and requires further research. In any event, it is a fact that the Book of Chronicles presents David's activities without mentioning the House of Saul even once.[21]

Support for these hypotheses may perhaps be found in 2 Sam. 7. Close scrutiny of that chapter will sharpen our perception of the tensions between the old and the new, and clarify the nature of the fundamental change the author ascribes to David.

to the period of the Second Temple, based on its language, its reflection of national and legal situations, and the views expressed in it.

Eichrodt, *Theologie* (1948), vol. 1 pp. 6–24; *Theology* (1961), vol. 1 pp. 36–39, believes that it was the Lord's promise about the permanence of His relationship to the royal house, that removed the constant fear of God's arbitrariness, a fear characteristic of pagan religions. In its place, an atmosphere of trust and security evolved.

20. Rost, *Thronnachfolge* (1926), p. 174; *Succession* (1982), p. 49, believes that the references to the house of Saul, as the complete opposite of the House of David (e.g., 2 Sam. 7:15: "I will not take my steadfast love from him, as I took it from Saul, ...") were written immediately after the fall of the Northern Kingdom, their rhetorical aim being to teach us that the Northern Kingdom was rejected just as the house of Saul had been. This is the way the editor-author, living in the 8th century, wrestled with problems of his time.
21. There are various ways of explaining why Saul's name is never mentioned in Chronicles. It may be because of the consistency with which the Chronist mentions the kings of Israel only in cases of contact with the kings of Judah. It is also possible that he saw no point in singling out the House of Saul as the antithesis of the house of David.

CHAPTER FOUR

DOES THE LORD 'DWELL IN A HOUSE' OR DOES HE 'MOVE ABOUT IN TENT AND TABERNACLE'? 2 Sam. 7

Approaches to the Story

The point of the whole story is quite clear, but it must be noted that the conflict — a requisite for any story — is here on two different levels. The first is obvious: David's wish to build a temple to God is rejected by the Deity. The second level depends upon how that rejection is interpreted. Medieval Jewish commentaries imply a covert conflict between the holiness of the Temple and David's prestige. On this there is a clear difference between traditional commentaries and modern research. Traditional commentaries unhesitatingly place the holiness of the Temple above the prestige of David, although it finds no contradiction between the two: ostensibly the honour due to David is beyond dispute, but for obvious reasons he is disqualified from building the Temple.[1] Biblical research agrees, in one form or another, mainly following

1. Levi ben Gershom, for example, states explicitly: "He should be content with the success he has achieved, and should not aspire to greater things, such as that the Temple be built by him." But the same idea appears in Rashi's commentary. He cites Haninah ben Saffa: "This man to whom I am sending you is known as a person given to making vows... Lest he say, 'I will neither eat nor drink until I have done so and so; and then I shall lose him." This is doubtless a hint that David's practical and direct approach does not necessarily make him suitable for the construction of the Temple (see *Yalkut Shimoni* 143:85).

the lead of Wellhausen,[2] that the narrative presents David in a messianic light, and the message it conveys goes something like this: David wants to build a house for the Lord — therefore the Lord will build a house for David.[3] Clearly, in this context the author is more concerned with the prestige and perpetuity of the House of David than with the holiness of the Temple. In other words, in this narrative the question of the Temple arises mainly as testimony to the status of the House of David.[4] Nathan's prophecy is regarded by modern scholars as the source of the belief in the eternal existence of the house of David.[5] In this prophecy David is assured the kingdom "for ever" (2 Sam. 7:13): the Lord's grace will never abandon him. But most scholars also stress the ideological tension reflected in this chapter,[6] tension focused on the refusal to respond favourably to David's desire to build an abode for the Lord. (The question as to why Nathan at first agreed with David's intention and only heard later what the Lord had to say on the subject is of secondary importance.) There is no agreement as to the meaning of the refusal or what it conveys, as will be discussed later. At this point I shall only note that to my mind this story, too, reflects the argument about the image or perception of the Deity. A god who refuses to 'stay at home' because he has been accus-

2. See Wellhausen, *Composition* (1889), p. 256, and a discussion on the structure of the text in Bleek, *Einleitung* (1878), p. 223.
3. Hertzberg, *Samuelbücher* (1960), pp. 197–200; *Samuel* (1964), pp. 240–244; Clements, *David* (1967), pp. 47–60. On the similarity between 2 Sam. 5 and Gen. 15 see ibid. p. 54 note 24.
4. McCarthy, "Deuteronomistic History" (1965).
5. Buber, *Königtum Gottes* (1932), pp. 178–179, deals with the positive attitude towards the kingdom in this prophecy, due to its ability to assure tranquility under the Lord's guidance. Uffenheimer, *Ancient Prophecy* (1973), pp. 155–164 concludes from the prophecy that the kingdom is perceived as the highest expression of divine grace towards Israel, and that the key expressions in the chapter — viz., the house, the throne, kingdom, forever and ever — hint that the kingdom of David is perceived as the highest achievement of the ancient kingdom of God and the epitome of its realization.
6. Schmidt, "Kritik" (1971).

tomed to 'wander around in Tent and Tabernacle' seems to me to reflect the adherence of the believers to an age old perception. They look upon David's desire to build a permanent dwelling for the Lord as a wish to uproot that perception, and this they fear. But Nathan's prophecy also sets out the ideological content of the new future; it is a response that includes the substance of the 'revolution' in religion.

Scholars generally agree that the text before us is not uniform, that there is inner tension among its components. Some attribute its present construction to a variety of sources,[7] while others maintain that it is a combination of several traditions[8] or of various editorial layers.[9] It is generally accepted, even by those who claim that basically the text is uniform,[10] that some Deuteronomistic additions or indications of Deuteronomistic editing can be discerned.

There is no agreement, however, as to the distribution of the various components with the exception of vs. 13 (all, or most of it) and the second half of vs. 11, about which agreement is virtually universal.

With regard to the refusal to accede to David's request, it is worth noting the approach of the traditional commentaries. In principle they are guided by their perception of uniformity: the refusal is mentioned several times in the Bible in different contexts. All the traditional commentaries (except Abrabanel) tend to inter-

7. See notes 34–43 below.
8. Sievers, *Samuel* (1907), and below notes 35 & 37.
9. Rost, *Thronnachfolge* (1926) pp. 159–183; *Succession* (1982), pp. 35–56; see also, Abramsky, *Kingdom* (1977) pp. 153–154.
10. McCarthy, "Deuteronomistic History" (1965). This is the view accepted today by most scholars. As far as I know, only two maintain that most of the material is uniform in style and written by one hand, and may even go back to David's own time. McKenzie, "Dynastic Oracle" (1947); Flanagan, Traditions (1970), p. 92.

pret all the references to it in the same way. Instead of "Would you build me a house to dwell in?" (2 Sam. 7:5), the parallel verse in 1 Chr. 17:4 reads: לא אתה "You shall not build me a house to dwell in" (and also the Septuagint to 2 Sam. 7:5). The difference is significant: from the structure of the sentence in Chronicles it appears that the Lord does not object to the basic idea of residing in a temple, but **David** is not to be the one to build it. The Samuel text conveys a different meaning: it can certainly be read with the emphasis on the "for me to dwell in", and not on the word "you".

In 1 Kings 5:17 [= RSV 5:3] Solomon tells Hiram, king of Tyre: "You know that David my father could not build a house for the name of the Lord his God because of the warfare with which his enemies surrounded him", and in Chronicles we are told that David, ordering Solomon to build a home for the deity, says to him: "But the word of the Lord came to me, saying, 'you have shed much blood and have waged great wars; you shall not build a house to my name, because you have shed so much blood before me upon the earth...'" (1 Chr. 22:8).

In view of the three passages cited above, the cause of the postponement would seem to be clear: David had shed blood, and is therefore disqualified from building the Temple, and this is stressed in the Lord's rhetorical question in 2 Sam. 7:5 "would you build me a house to dwell in?" which leads commentators to emphasize the word "you".[11] At the same time one notes that in the

11. Joseph Kara: "Not you." But Abrabanel, referring to the tone of chastisement in the text ("Why does the blessed Lord chastise him asking: 'Will you build my house?'"), comments: "This is meant to explain that David was prevented from building the Temple not because he was blameworthy and spilled the enemy's blood, which was not held against him but was rather in his favour. There was another reason... the Lord saw that the time was inappropriate for building the Temple."
On the other hand Driver, *Notes* (1913), pp. 231–232, prefers the Chronicler's version of "You shall not" (1 Chr. 17:4). Likewise Segal, *Samuel* (1956), p. 276, although he stresses the general positive attitude of the chapter towards David, explains this sentence as a purely rhetorical question.

traditional commentaries this spilling of blood does not imply wrongdoing. It is accepted as a fact and inevitable (Abrabanel). Solomon refers to these matters in a very matter-of-fact way in his speech of blessing at the dedication of the Temple. He tells in his own words of his father's desire to build it, and the Lord's refusal to allow him to do so: "nevertheless you shall not build the house, but your son who shall be born to you shall build the house for my name" (1 Kings 8:19).

It seems to me, however, that the version in Chronicles (and Kings) does not mean exactly the same as the Samuel version: the events are related with the image of Solomon, not David, before the writer, and he must present matters in a way appropriate to his needs. In other words, Solomon, who is interested in presenting the Temple as a symbol of the highest order of sanctity, is obligated to explain why it was not built in his father's day. But the reason that serves Solomon's interest does not present a useful contribution to David's image. In my opinion, we must interpret the question in the Samuel version with stress on the words "for me to dwell in"[12] and not "shalt thou".

It thus becomes clear that the Lord's question expresses the theological problem. It is directed against David's desire to place the Deity in a temple, not against him personally. The problem is not whether David is fit for the task or not, but rather the task itself. Therefore, if we conclude that the Chronicler's version is the correct one (not you) then the inclination of the Samuel version will stand out even more clearly, and this may be an intentional

2 Sam. 7 MT no doubt was subjected to later redactions. This is especially true of vs. 13, which combines MT with 1 Chron. 17:12: "He shall build a house for me, and I will establish his throne for ever." The Septuagint of 2 Sam. 7:13 reads: Αὐτὸς οἰκοδομήσει μοι, οἶκον τῷ ὀνόματί μου, καὶ ἀνορθώσω τὸν θρόνον αὐτοῦ ἕως εἰς τὸν αἰῶνα, see Talmon, "Textual Study" (1975).

12. McCarter, *II Samuel* (1984), p. 198, believes that the interrogative form "would you" [= האתה] is in opposition to "me" [לי].

change.[13] In other words, the text means to stress the question of whether it is indeed possible for the Deity to be confined within walls,[14] with all such a change may imply from a theological point of view. If this is the correct interpretation, this is the central conflict in the story. However, this calls for close scrutiny. In my opinion there are signs of tension in the words of David and of Nathan. This tension centres in juxtaposing concepts of permanence and transience in everything pertaining to comprehension of the Divine ways and the relationship between the Lord and the rulers. This requires an examination of the text and its structure.[15]

2 Samuel 7: Text and Composition

The main difficulties one encounters in studying this text are the following:

(a) From vs. 8 onwards there is no mention of the Ark, whereas in the opening verses the fate of the Ark is the cause of the entire

13. One can clearly see the deliberate re-working of the text in MT, in two ways: (a) An expression "אשר יהיה", used in a rare sense, i.e. = to give birth, as in 1 Chron. 17:11 and in the Septuagint to 2 Sam. 7:12, was replaced by the more common one, "אשר יצא", i.e., will come forth. (b) In 2 Sam. 7:13 there are signs of editing in the spirit of Deuteronomy in the replacement of "to me" by "to my name." This can be seen clearly by comparing MT of Chronicles 17:12 "he shall build a house for me" with the Septuagint of 2 Sam. 7:13. See Talmon, "Textual Study" (1975); Seeligmann, "Text" (1979), pp. 265–266.
14. On the statement "I have not dwelt in a house," see the survey in McCarter, *II Samuel* (1984), p. 199. He claims that this verse contradicts 1 Sam. 1:7, and that either there is an intention in 2 Sam. 7 to erase the memory of Shilo, or else the various names given the Shilo temple in 1 Sam. 1–3 are anachronisms. In any event, there is a clear contradiction between the verse we are dealing with and 1 Sam. 1:7. But he does not think there is any contradiction between ישב (dwell) and שכן (live).
15. Von Rad, *Theologie* (1958), vol. 1 p. 69; *Theology* (1962), vol. 1 p. 60 believes that in this situation it is Nathan who represents the nomadic ideal, which includes "tabernacle" and "tent." But in his opinion, the identity of the object represented by this concept is not certain.

story.[16] As David puts it, "See now, I dwell in a house of cedar, but the ark of God dwells in a tent" (2 Sam. 7:2).

(b) Verse 5 speaks of building a house for the Lord, "Would you build me a house to dwell in?", whereas vs. 13 speaks of building a house to His name "He shall build a house for my name", and according to vs. 2, the house is intended for the Ark.[17]

(c) Verse 13 presents difficulties for several reasons: 1. From the point of view of content, since it presumably deals with Solomon and his life's work, it is generally considered a later addition.[18] 2. From the point of view of language, there is an unorthodox use of the Hebrew root כו"ן (*kwn*) instead of the usual active causative form of the same verb as in vs. 12 והכינותי "and I will establish". 3. The duplication of vss. 12b and 13b: in vs. 12b "who shall come forth from your body and I will establish his kingdom"; in vs. 13b "and I will establish the throne of his kingdom for ever". 4. David's prayer of thanksgiving makes no mention whatever of what is said in vs. 13a.[19]

(d) Verse 12 speaks of "your offspring" whereas vs. 11b speaks of "a house". Therefore some commentators assume that vs. 11b was not written by the author of vss. 8–11b, 12, 14.[20] The transition to the third person in the middle of vs. 11 "the Lord declares to you" seems to support this claim: until now the Lord always spoke of himself in the first person.

(e) There is some inconsistency between the words of prophecy and the content of the thanksgiving prayer (especially in vss. 25–

16. Rost, *Thronnachfolge* (1926), pp. 159–183; *Succession* (1982), pp. 35–56.
17. Rost, *Thronnachfolge* (1926), p. 167; *Succession* (1982), p. 42.
18. See below, notes 34–36 & 38.
19. Thenius, *Bücher Samuels* (1842), p. 145; Nowack, *Samuelis* (1902), p. 178.
20. Tiktin, *Untersuchungen* (1922), p. 48; Rost, *Thronnachfolge* (1926), p. 170; *Succession* (1982), p. 44.

29). David is asking for things that the Lord had already promised him explicitly (vss. 13, 16), which leads some commentators to believe[21] that the author of vss. 25–29 was unfamiliar with the verses containing the promise. This means that vss. 13 and 16 are later additions. See below with reference to the expression עד עולם (for ever).

(f) The idea expressed in vs. 14 about the Lord's unconditional benevolence is extraordinary for a biblical story from the period of the Monarchy.[22]

(g) Biblical research tends to distinguish between concepts that were current in ancient times and terms and concepts that were characteristic of the Deuteronomistic or Priestly editing. Obviously there is no general agreement about these expressions, and each merits separate scrutiny.

הניח לו (had given him rest, vs. 1) is probably a Deuteronomistic phrase.[23]

מתהלך באהל ובמשכן (moving about in a tent for my dwelling, vs. 6). It is customary to interpret the root הל"ך (*hlk*) in its various forms (vs. 6 ואהיה מתהלך and vs. 7 התהלכתי) as implying the constant presence of the Deity. Hence the expression not only conveys an awareness of the tradition of the tabernacle in the desert,[24] but also implies that divine providence runs through all history.

21. Tsevat, "House of David" (1965).
22. Tsevat, "House of David" (1965). His claim does not agree with Gen. 15. Furthermore Clements, *David* (1967), points out the resemblance between Gen. 15 and 2 Sam. 7. On the idea of adoption in vs. 14a, see: North, "Kingship" (1932); Brin, "Formula" (1972).
23. Deuteronomy 3:20; 12:10; 25:19; Joshua 1:13,15; 21:44; 1 Kings 5:18. See also McCarthy, "Deuteronomistic History" (1965).
24. Loewenstamm, "Tabernacle" (1968).

This perception is strengthened if we assume that Tent and Tabernacle are not merely synonims,[25] but actually suggest a distinction between the stages in which the sanctuary was constructed: from the most ancient form of a tent to the later wooden structure, i.e., a tabernacle.[26] In other words, historical perspective is reflected here.

נגיד (prince, vs. 8). The exact meaning of this term and the reason for Nathan's use of it here, when David is indisputably accepted as king by all, is controversial. Most scholars believe this is an ancient title, going as far back as the time of the Judges.[27] Others maintain that it marks the transition from the period of the Judges to the Kingdom.[28] Only a minority consider it a Deuteronomistic expression.[29] Whatever its exact meaning (to me it seems to describe a potential king, before he becomes one in fact), there appears to be something ephemeral about it.

עד עולם (for ever, vss. 13 and 16). This is almost the opposite of נגיד (prince). While נגיד implies impermanence (one is not נגיד all his life, but only until he is crowned), עד עולם relates to a dimension of time that can only imply stability.[30]

25. Abramski, *Kingdom* (1977), pp. 153–154.
26. Milgrom, *Terminology* (1970), p. 68, especially note 249. His assumption that the expression "tent and tabernacle" contains a historical perspective is based mainly on the context, which includes the words 'servant' and 'my servant' (2 Sam. 7:5, 8, 19, 20 etc.), since 'servant' refers only to tabernacle worship. McCarter, *II Samuel* (1984), p. 200 disagrees, arguing that the expression is used mainly to emphasize the Lord's freedom of action, i.e., freedom against the tendency to bind the deity to a particular location.
27. For a review of this subject see Soggin, *Königtum* (1967), passim; Liver, "Nagid" (1968); Weisman, Charisma (1972).
28. Albright, *Samuel* (1961), passim.
29. Carlson, *David* (1964), pp. 97–128, passim.
30. Alt, "Königtum" (1951); "Monarchy" (1968). At the same time Jeremias, "Lade" (1971), notes that the term נגיד (prince) could be applied to David only as the person in charge of the Ark.
For more on the term נגיד in this context, see Gese, "Davidsbund" (1964); Richter, "Nagid" (1965).

It is worth noting that evidence of Deuteronomic thinking is to be found in vss. 6 and 23, for the following reasons: a) The way the Exodus is referred to in Joshua-Kings, is characteristic of the Deuteronomist. b) Great importance is attached to the Exodus, as in vs. 23, where it is mentioned as one of the constitutive events. c) The editor-author juxtaposes the Exodus with the choice of David and the construction of the Temple. This is characteristic of the tendency of the Deuteronomists "to fuse the Jerusalem traditions, such as the House of David, the Temple, and Mount Zion, with a Northern tradition, such as the Exodus".[31] This tendency began in Judah towards the end of the Monarchy and came to its full expression during the Exile, when the Deuteronomistic historiography assumed its final form.

It should also be borne in mind that it was typical of Deuteronomistic writers[32] to weave speeches into their historical narrative, particularly the speeches of leaders, men of God or prophets.

There are many theories about the way this chapter came into being and its meaning.[33] As far as composition and structure are concerned there are some who maintain that the material consists mainly of early elements, to which a number of sentences were added by the Deuteronomist.[34] Others hold that it was the other way round, i.e., most of the material is Deuteronomistic.[35] Accord-

31. Hoffman, *Exodus* (1983), pp. 150, 152, 186.
32. Noth, *Studien* (1943), pp. 4–6; Weinfeld, *Deuteronomy* (1972), pp. 10–58.
33. For the meaning of the prophecy and its time, see Carlson, *David* (1964), pp. 98–127, and especially his bibliography.
34. Bleek, *Einleitung* (1878), p. 223, argues that verses 5b and 11a-13a were originally consecutive, and were placed in the extended version by a later redaction. Procksch, "David" (1913) presents the counter-argument that vss. 11b-12 together with 4a, 5b and perhaps also 14a, 18 & 27, are of very early origin.
35. Sievers, *Samuel* (1907), thinks that the chapter contains material from an earlier version of Nathan's prophecy, i.e., vss. 11 & 16b. Kittel, *Geschichte* (1923), p. 123 thinks that the material is mainly Deuteronomistic, but that most

ing to another theory two old sources were combined by the Deuteronomist who also added some verses of his own.[36] Still another suggestion is that the story was formed in various stages, the Deuteronomistic layer being only one of them.[37] Finally, there

verses contain earlier kernels. Weiser, "Tempelbaukrise" (1965) deals with the difficulties and inconsistencies in vss. 10b-11a, 12–13 and 24–25.

36. Budde, *Samuelbücher* (1902), pp. 232–235; *Samuel* (1894), pp. 82–83. His hypothesis is based mainly on the discrepancy between vss. 5 and 11 (see above note 34). The view of Ruprecht, *Tempel* (1977), p. 63 is similar. McCarter, *II Samuel* (1984), pp. 196–197, too, maintains that the unification of material from the different sources was accomplished by the Deuteronomistic redaction, which may have been preceded by an earlier one. In his opinion it is difficult to suppose that the author of vs. 3 also wrote vss. 5–7. He believes that vs. 3 belongs to the oldest stratum of the narrative, that its approach was accepted by the Deuteronomist. But the approach which negates the building of the Temple, as expressed in vss. 5–7, is of later origin than vs. 3.
Tiktin, *Untersuchungen* (1922), p. 48 divides the sources differently. He does not believe that vs. 11b was written by the author of vss. 8–11a, 12, 14.

37. So thinks Gressmann, *Geschichtsschreibung* (1910), p. 138. In his opinion, the editor-author added a poetic oracle, which he rendered into prose, to narrative material of much earlier origin, and then appended David's prayer.
Rost, *Thronnachfolge* (1926), pp. 159–183; *Succession* (1982), pp. 35–36, believes that the material contains three main parts or layers (vss. 1–7, 8–17 and vss. 23–29). However, each layer contains sub-layers. Nathan's prophecy consists of three such sublayers. The first dates back to David's time, and in this respect Rost agrees with Sievers as to vss. 11 & 16–17 (see above, note 35). Its main purpose is to ensure internal security and to turn the kingdom's main effort from expanding its frontiers to assuring its internal stability. The second layer centres on the divine promise that the Lord's loving kindness will never be removed from David, as it was from Saul. In his opinion these words hint at the kingdom of Judah, as distinct from the Northern Kingdom, and this layer dates to the period after the fall of Samaria. The third layer dates back to the time of Josiah. The oldest, most basic components of the three layers are to be found in vss. 1–7, 11–12, 16 and 18–21.
Noth, *DHistory* (1981), pp. 54–62, agrees with this division, and emphasizes that the first addition to these verses, which precedes the Deuteronomistic layer, consists of vss. 13a, 19, 20 and 22–24.
Von Rad, *Theologie* (1958), vol. 1 p. 48 note 47; *Theology* (1962), vol. 1 p. 39 note 47 too believes that the earliest nucleus consists of the verses indicated by Rost, and adds that in the latest layer, the accent is on David's descendants, while in

are a few who hold that all the material comes from a single ancient source, perhaps going back as far as David,[38] but this theory is not widely accepted.

In light of this survey I would like to point out that:

a) What has come down to us is the result of repeated redaction: the story of David's desire to build a house for the Lord and Nathan's response was originally much shorter.

b) Scholars vary in their reconstruction of the different strata of the story.[39] They agree only that all or part of vs. 13 is a late addition.

c) There is, however, a consensus that one of the central ideas of the chapter is the message that it is not David who will build a

vss. 22–24 the emphasis is on extending the object of the divine promise from the king to the entire people as 'the eternal people.'
Abramsky, *Kingdom* (1977), p. 149 also thinks that the material consists of layers, but in his opinion, the words of David were composed later than Nathan's prophecy, which includes earlier, pre-Deuteronomistic components.

38. Kaufmann, "David" (1957). In his opinion the chapter contains no later additions, not even vs. 13, which contains no explicit mention of Solomon.
Uffenheimer, *Ancient Prophecy* (1973), pp. 155–164 does not accept the identification of expressions such as הניח לו (=had given him rest) as Deuteronomistic. Vss. 10–11, he maintains, reflect national pride, which suits the early days of David's rule, and vss. 12, 13, 15, 26 and 29 also reflect the situation prior to the partition of the kingdom, when the kingdom of David is viewed as the crowning achievement of the kingdom of God.
McKenzie, "Dynastic Oracle" (1947) believes that the materials are historically authentic, virtually uniform, and possibly dating from the time of David. Flanagan, Traditions (1970), pp. 48, 92, holds a similar view.

39. The clearest disagreement is over the passage from vs. 8 onwards. Rost, *Thronnachfolge* (1926), pp. 159–183; *Succession* (1982), pp. 35–56 maintains that it was written by the author of the Succession Narrative. Eissfeldt, *Komposition* (1931), pp. 138–139 differs. In his opinion, the passage belongs to the basic material of the chapter.

house for the Lord, but the Lord who will build a house for David.[40] Verses 13 and 11b are of vital importance to the structure of the chapter in its present form.[41] The same holds true for the relationship between the various parts of the chapter. David's prayer and above all vs. 19: "thou hast spoken also of thy servant's house for a great while to come" which is generally regarded as early,[42] can only be interpreted as a reaction to the words of Nathan in vss. 8–16. If we were to separate vss. 1–16 from the rest of the chapter, they would constitute a story about the final and unequivocal rejection of David — someting that is not only alien to the context, but also fails to provide any basis for David's words (vss. 18–29).

Thus the problem of the chapter's composition requires a different approach.

It seems to me that there is tension between two main sets of expressions. This accords with the two perceptions — the old and the new — that constitute the conflict of the story. The two sets are divided more-or-less symmetrically between the two parts of the chapter.[43] One denotes impermanence, instability, wandering and open spaces, while the other implies stability and permanence. The former focuses on attitudes to the past, the latter relates to the future. By 'expressions' I mean in addition to words and combinations of words, illustrative definitions (see table on pp. 105–107).

40. Wellhausen, *Composition* (1889), p. 257; von Rad, *Theologie* (1958), vol. 1 p. 308; *Theology* (1962), vol. 1 p. 310.

41. Rost, *Thronnachfolge* (1926), p. 167; *Succession* (1982), p. 42.

42. Mainly Procksch, "David" (1913), pp. 122–124; McKenzie, "Dynastic Oracle" (1947); Flanagan, Traditions (1970), p. 92.

43. Mettinger, *King and Messiah* (1976), pp. 158, 167, 174, 267 thinks that Nathan's prophecy reflects stages in the development of the concept of king and kingdom from the charismatic ideas and the idea of adoption to the Divine promise of eternity for the dynasty. He bases his view on the term נגיד (prince) in its various connotations, and on 'making a name'. Only vss. 1b & 10–11, he claims, are later additions. As to the structure of the text see ibidem pp. 51–52.

One set includes the expressions: יריעה (curtains, tent vs. 2), מתהלך (moving about, vs. 6), התהלכתי (have moved, vs. 7), הלכת (went, vs. 9), הלכו (went, vs. 23), אהל ומשכן (tent and tabernacle, vs. 6), לרעות (to shepherd, vs. 7 — for discussion of this verse see pp. 92–93 below), מן הנוה (from the pasture, vs. 8), מאחר הצאן (from following the sheep), נגיד (prince, vs. 8). Perhaps one ought to include here בני עולה (wicked, vs. 10), יסור (depart, vs. 15), הסירותי (removed, vs. 15); and because of its connotation of intimacy also אני אהיה לו לאב והוא יהיה לי לבן (I will be his father, and he shall be my son, vs. 14).[44]

Expressions that belong to the second set are: הניח, והניחותי (rest, given rest, vss. 1, 11), יש"ב in its various forms: ישב, יושב, לשבתי, ישבתי (dwell, vss. 1, 2, 5, 6), בית (house, vss. 1, 2, 5, 6, 7, 11, 13, 16, 18, 19, 25, 26, 27, 29) ונטעתיו (plant, vs. 10), שכן תחתיו (dwell in their own place, vs. 10), ולא ירגז עוד (be disturbed no more vs. 10), והקימותי (raise up, vs. 12); כו"ן in its various forms: והכינותי (establish, vs. 12), וכננתי (establish, vs. 13), ותכונן (confirmed vs. 24), נכון (established, vs. 26); כסא – ממלכה (throne of kingdom, vs. 13); עד עולם, לעולם (forever, vss. 16, 24, 25, 26, 29); נאמן (ביתך) (shall be established vs. 16).

All these expressions are charged with meanings beyond their lexical value. Some of them, because of their context, at least appear as *termini technici.* Others have associative connotations.

"I took you from the pasture, from following the sheep" (2 Sam. 7:8). It stands to reason that this formulation is meant to convey more than its literal meaning. Clearly, the Lord does not intend to remind David of his humble past in order 'to put him in his place' and ensure that he will be satisfied with modest demands, as was the case with Jeroboam. Jeroboam was told: "Because I exalted you

44. This text implies the idea of adoption, and would seem to tie in with the charismatic concept of the kingdom. See Alt, "Königtum" (1951); "Monarchy" (1968), and recently also Brin, "Formula" (1972), particularly note 9.

from among the people" (1 Kings 14:7), and Baasha was told: "Since I exalted you out of the dust" (1 Kings 16:2). The difference is striking. In the case of the latter two there is the word יען (forasmuch, because, since) which does not appear in the text of 2 Sam. 7. In Kings we have הרימותיך (I exalted), whereas in Samuel the word is לקחתיך (I took). As I understand it הרימותיך implies raising someone from a lowly position and therefore a degrading expression; whereas לקחתיך has positive connotations of choosing. Thus even when the same formula is used, David is not belittled.

Since David was taken from the נוה (sheepcote) it is clear that whatever was symbolized by נוה will be taken into the נגיד[ות] (princehood). Furthermore, in addition to what is suggested by the phrase "from following the sheep" the context shows that here too political leadership is conceived as shepherding "whom I commanded to shepherd my people Israel (2 Sam. 7:7).

The words "the tribes/judges of Israel, whom I commanded to shepherd my people Israel" are also pregnant with meaning. There is here a textual difficulty. Most scholars prefer to read שפטי (judges) rather than שבטי (tribes) as in 1 Chronicles 17:6, even though there the Septuagint is like MT in 2 Sam. 7:7.[45] But regardless of how we read the text,[46] emended or not, the meaning is still the same, i.e., leadership was handed down from tribe to tribe in accordance with a divine plan (especially in view of the emphasis on "in all places where I have moved").

2 Sam. 7: Ideas and Meaning

The reference to the past in the Lord's words contains a complete ideological perception. Opposition to the construction of

45. McCarter, *II Samuel* (1984), p. 200 reads שבטי (my tribe), but interprets it נושאי שבט.

46. For a discussion of the subject see Barthélemy, *Critique Textuelle* (1982), pp. 245–246. The reading שבטי (=tribes) is based on Deut. 29:9, in comparison with Joshua 23:2 and 24:1. See also Gen. 49:16.

the House of the Lord stems from the fact that placing the Deity in a house conflicts with the ideology implicit in "moving about", "shepherding" and all relevant terms (tent and tabernacle, sheep-cote etc.).

It is conceived as a revolutionary act conflicting with the traditional concepts of the deity, "dwell" rather than "wander about"; and with leadership "throne", rather than "sheepcote, pasture" and apparently also נגיד "prince".

It can be assumed that ideological tension of this sort may surface in different ways. It may express itself in a single initiative or in response to an act such as the declaration of the mere intention to build a temple. Indeed, some see here the main motive for telling the story, for internal purposes,[47] possibly even under the influence of foreign traditions.[48] Such tension may result from a series of acts, a comprehensive political process, in this case — by bringing up the Ark to Jerusalem — purchasing the Araunah threshing floor, and declaring the intention to build a temple. Some maintain that this was the sequence of events, and that from a historical point of view, Nathan's prophecy belongs after the story about the purchase of the threshing floor.[49] But tension of

47. Kaufmann, *Religion* (1947), pp. 358–359 maintains that building the Temple calls for a great national effort, and Nathan's words express the apprehension that the time is not yet ripe for it. See the words of Abrabanel, note 11 above.

48. Ota, "Note" (1974) deals with the strict attitude that prevailed in the ancient Near East towards any construction of extensive repairs to sanctuaries. The stories of Godea, Assarhadon and Nabonaid reveal the apprehension that preceded the issue of a permit to reconstruct the Temple. Whoever received the approval of the gods for such an undertaking spoke of it with pride. Hints of a refusal to grant such a permit are contained in the Sumeric poem "The Curse of Akkad", where Naram-Sin fails to get Enlil's permission to renovate a sanctuary.
On the construction of sanctuaries as the special obligation of the king as an expression of his loyalty to the gods, see Bickerman, "Cyrus" (1964).

49. Segal, *Samuel* (1956), p. 276.

this kind between concepts can also result from traumatic experiences such as the division of the monarchy, or the fall of Samaria, or may last for prolonged historical periods like the separate kingdoms.

One may surmise that in the course of the transmutations of the text, various editors actualized the message through the use of contemporary expressions. Though all of this is little more than guesswork, it nevertheless seems to me to offer the best explanation of the differences between the layers of this text.

There is no generally accepted definition and reconstruction of the strata of this story as there is in other biblical narratives.[50] However, I think it should be stressed that the seminal core must have included the following aspects, which can be gleaned from the present text:

a) The apprehension about David's initiative could not have been amorphous[51] but must have indicated ideological resistance to the anticipated changes. There must have been special concern about traditions and rites which might be done away with. Since one of the sets of expressions centers on the past and the other on the future, one could say that the tension is between the old and the new. Otherwise it is enough to say that the tension is between two different perceptions.[52]

b) The story must have expressed apprehension; but also an attempt to allay it.

50. See Weisman, *Jacob* (1986), pp. 41–48; 57–94, on the way the Jacob stories reached their final form.
51. For an example of insufficiently defined apprehension see Kaufmann, *Religion* (1947), pp. 358–359: "an apprehension lest the hour of a great national effort may not yet have arrived." On ancient traditions disapproving of the building of new sanctuaries, see above notes 47 & 48.
52. For a discussion of this subject, see McCarter, *II Samuel* (1984), p. 199.

Without these two attributes, there could hardly have been a story, and it is difficult to understand its ideological contribution to the complex of the David stories.

2 Sam. 7: Past and Future

In the following part of the analysis I shall deal with the story in its present form alone. The present structure of the chapter, in which central expressions are almost symmetrically divided, (see table on p. 105) may support my assumption that the same expressions have the same meaning throughout the chapter. Thus, since vss. 23–24 explicitly present the Exodus as a constitutive event,[53] that was probably also the meaning of the Exodus in vs. 6.

Therefore, the Lord's declaration that from the day he brought Israel out of Egypt he has known no rest but has been wandering in tent and Tabernacle is a statement that the wanderings are his most fundamental characteristic, identified with the God of the Covenant.

Verse 7 again states clearly that this wandering among the children of Israel was a basic attribute of the Lord, who was with the people of Israel all through their pre-monarchic history. Moreover, this history has been guided by the Lord, who commanded the leaders of the people in every generation.[54] And since the rhetorical question "did I speak a word with any of..." appears in a context that regards history as being formed and directed by the Lord, it becomes clear that it was not by chance that He did not order His house to be built. The Lord deliberately refrained from doing so i.e., the building of a temple conflicted with His plan of history.

53. On the tendency to see the making of the people as an event rather than a process, see Licht, "Establishment" (1980).

54. This interpretation is correct, whether we accept the reading שבטי (tribes) or שפטי (judges). See above note 46.

Some scholars think that vs. 8 introduces a new unit or stratum.[55] Whether this is so or not, it clarifies the intention of the Divine plans for David: "I took you from the pasture from following the sheep, that you should be prince over my people Israel" (2 Sam. 7:8). As the structure is parallel to the previous passage (vss. 6–7), it is reasonable to conclude that just as the Exodus is considered as a constitutive event, here the pasture is the main essence of princehood.

Vss. 8–10 also convey the idea that the divine intention has been realized throughout history: "and I have been with you wherever you went" (2 Sam. 7:9), and the result was: "and have cut off all your enemies from before you" (2 Sam. 7:9).[56] These words refer to the past and they belong together with the opening "and the Lord had given him rest from all his enemies round about" (vs. 1) whereby the circle is also closed structurely. Vss. 1–10 refer to and support the tradition of wandering and everything relating to the past. From here onwards, the future is being revealed. It is a kind of response to the misgivings that have given rise to the whole story.

Nevertheless the story does not seem to me to contain any pledge of a compromise of the old tradition with the new. This is not Weiser's view. He believes that the story's purpose is to present the future temple as a place for the worship of the God of the theophany of Sinai. According to Weiser this provides the assurance that the Temple is not the dwelling place of the Deity, but a ritualistic transformation of God's revelation on Sinai.[57] In other words, this ensures that the Temple will absorb and combine within it the entire Sinai tradition.

55. Rost, *Thronnachfolge* (1926), p. 167; *Succession* (1982), p. 42.
56. From the second half of 2 Sam. 7:9 "and I will make for you a great name" onwards we note the turning away from the past towards the promises of the future.
57. Weiser, "Tempelbaukrise" (1965).

I do not believe that the story in 2 Sam. 7 relates to the Sinai tradition, nor do I intend to deal here with the relationship between the traditions of the Exodus and of Sinai.[58] Although there is a connection between the Sinai Covenant and the Kingdom of David in Pslams 89 and 132, which contain a clear reference to the words of Nathan, there is no such connection in 2 Sam. 7.[59] Nor do I think the message of the latter to be that David intended to integrate the tribal traditions in his kingdom.[60]

It therefore seems to me that the text presents no compromise, but rather a confrontation, favouring the permanent over the "walking about".[61]

58. Von Rad, *Hexateuch* (1938); "Hexateuch" (1966) accepts the version of Galling, *Erwählungstraditionen* (1928), according to whom the tradition of the Exodus evolved separately from the tradition of Sinai, in different sanctuaries, and only cult bound the two together. Von Rad believes that the Exodus tradition crystallized at Gilgal, and the Sinai tradition in Shechem. For a survey of the two traditions see Nicholson, *Exodus* (1973).
59. In Psalm 89:25–37 the relations between David and the Lord are defined as a covenant (see also vs. 40). This expression has formed the basis of many agreements that this Psalm is a later commentary on 2 Sam. 7. Von Rad, "Königsritual" (1947); "Royal Ritual" (1966), maintains that the passage contains material from very early sources, and the expression 'covenant' is not necessarily a late one, since it appears in "David's last words" (2 Sam. 23:5), which undoubtedly is a very ancient text.
According to von Rad Psalm 132 is also of early origin.
Schmidt, "Kritik" (1971), believes that Psalm 89 quotes Nathan, but makes use of Deuteronomistic terminology. The same applies to Psalm 132, which combines the two main motifs of 2 Sam. 7, and sharpens them: the desire to build a house for the Lord is expressed in the form of a vow, and the Divine promise as an oath.
For further discussion of the relation between 2 Sam 7 and Ps. 89 see Sarna "Psalm 89" (1963).
On the connection between various psalms and poetic oracles, see Bellinger, *Psalmody and Prophecy* (1984).
60. For a presentation of David's actions as intended to integrate traditions, see Cross, *Canaanite Myth* (1974), pp. 264–266.
61. That permanence is preferable to the impermanence of "wandering about", can also be gathered from the references to the relationship between the Lord and David in other sources. See especially Ps. 89, and note 59 above.

The promise that "the Lord will build you a house" is presented as the result of planning, in the same way as the historical processes were presented in vss. 1–7. According to vs. 11 'God has told'[62] that a house will be built for David. This implies that the organization and leadership in the period preceeding the monarchy were only a phase in a plan, the purpose of which was kingship. Ultimately God will build a house for David בית לדוד. Thus there is here no idealization of the past. It emerges from the text that the stages leading to this purpose of making a house are: making David's name great, establishing a permanent place for the people of Israel, as a result of which "I will appoint a place for my people Israel, and will plant them, that they may dwell in their own place, and be disturbed no more; and violent men shall afflict them no more" (vs. 10).

An unequivocal interpretation of the second part of this verse is difficult, but the first part is clear enough: it contains three different expressions implying permanence "and be disturbed no more; and violent men shall afflict them no more, as formerly".[63] Permanence is part of the final aim, so that "be disturbed no more" and "violent men shall afflict them no more" (vs. 10).

The context may lead one to interpret רג"ז (be disturbed) as being, in a certain sense, the opposite of the previous phrases. This enables us to accept, at least on general lines, an interpretation such as Carlson's, for whom the root רג"ז represents the anxiety of

62. Greenberg, "Religion" (1979), pp. 79, 82, notes that in these expressions, we can see the beginning of the perception of the kingdom of David as a means whereby the Lord will keep his covenant with Israel. At the same time he points out that messianic expectations were imputed to the kings of Northern Israel long before they were attributed to the House of David. See 2 Kings 13:17, and also the words of Jonah ben Amittai to Yoash king of Israel about his son Jeroboam (2 Kings 14:25). Even the concept, "the day of the Lord" originated, according to Greenberg, in the period of the wars with the Arameans.

63. For the use of the verb 'to dwell' to imply permanence, as understood by the Deuteronomist, see Noth, "Jerusalem" (1950).

one who was uprooted from his land.[64] The context also supports Kaufmann's view that "violent men" (vs. 10) refers to the difficulties during the time of the Judges.[65]

> With this in mind, one can perhaps regard the second half of vs. 9 as a kind of balancing transition from past to the future. I am referring to the promise "and I will make you a great name, like the name of the great ones of the earth" (vs. 9). It may be that the word גדולים (great ones) is a kind of term that was used in the period preceeding the kingdom, to imply elevated status, or nobility.[66] If that is so, the passage contains a hint that in his new status, David will inherit the seat of his predecessors. This supposition gains in strength from the use of the root גד"ל in David's prayer.

However, the climax of Nathan's prophecy, and therefore probably also the main thrust of its message, is to be found in the passage about the future of the House of David (vss. 12–16, especially vss. 14–15).

Verse 13 expresses a central idea of the entire chapter, namely, that as a reward for David's wish to build a house for the Lord, the Lord will build a house for David. Various signs however indicate that in the present context, the eternity of the House of David is more important for the author than sanctity of the Temple.[67] The

64. The interpretation of the verb רג"ז as conveying the fear of those who have been uprooted from their land, is not necessarily connected with the Exile. Carlson, *David* (1964), pp. 52–58 bases himself on Deut. 2:25 and 28:65.
65. Kaufmann, *Religion* (1947), p. 162.
66. In interpreting גדול as high-born, McCarter, *II Samuel* (1984), p. 201, bases himself on 2 Sam. 3:38.
67. Rost, *Thronnachfolge* (1926), pp. 179–180; *Succession* (1982), p. 51 has a different opinion as to the order of preferences. He believes that the Temple was so important to the author that in his view, granting permission to build it deserved a separate prophecy.

structure indicates that this idea is the climax of the chapter. It also describes historical events in such a way as to present the 'eternal House of David' as the culmination of events that began with the Exodus.

The structure of the passage (vss. 12–16) also supports the interpretation that the relations between the Lord and David are defined in vss. 14–15, but the verses on either side of them speak of the stability and eternity of the House of David (11b, 12, 13b, 16). Verse 15 also speaks of these stating that the bond between the seed of David and the Lord,[68] based on divine grace, will be eternal.[69]

The main attributes of the promised House of David are its being נאמן (firm establishment), נכון (stability and permanence), עד עולם (eternity).[70] These attributes are diametrically opposed to those that characterized earlier periods.

The Future

The focal point of the whole passage dealing with the future (vss. 9b-16) is contained in vss. 14–15. These describe the nature of the bond from the standpoint of the Deity, enumerating his obligations. This is also the quintessence of the theological aspect of the story.

68. In this study I do not differentiate between "offspring" (vs. 12) and "house" (vs. 13), as Rost, *Thronnachfolge* (1926), p. 179; *Succession* (1982), p. 51 does.
69. See the discussion above, Chapter Three note 19 and Eichrodt, *Theologie* (1948), vol. 1 pp. 6–24; *Theology* (1961), vol. 1 pp. 36–69. Also see von Rad, *Theologie* (1958), vol. 1 pp. 52, 59; *Theology* (1962), vol. 1 pp. 44, 55–56. But in his opinion the question of the Divine promise of the eternity of the House of David did not permeate biblical literature to the same extent as did the ideas of Divine choice in the Exodus.
70. Rost, *Thronnachfolge* (1926), pp. 170, 174; *Succession* (1982), pp. 44, 47 notes the duplication between vs. 11b (12) and vs. 13, and maintains, as does Sievers, *Samuel* (1907), passim. and Tiktin, *Untersuchungen* (1922), p. 48 that verses 11b and 16 constitute the oldest stratum in this passage.

The promise as formulated in vs. 14: "I will be his father, and he shall be my son", no doubt contains an echo of the formula of adoption. It is generally assumed that it is influenced by royal Egyptian texts.[71] Furthermore, the verse is interpreted as refering to messianic ideas, in the Bible and thereafter, and it is generally considered to be the source of the appelation "Son of God" for the Messiah.

In the parallel passage in Chronicles (1 Chr. 17:13), the second half of the verse is omitted, perhaps because the author of Chronicles does not allow himself to assume that God's chosen one could be considered a sinner, "when he comits iniquity",[72] or perhaps because the author wishes to stress the absolute nature of the divine promise.[73] Elsewhere in Chronicles, the expressison והוא יהיה לי לבן ואני אהיה לו לאב is interpreted literally (1 Chr. 22:9–10; 28:6). However, even if we assume that its source is an imported formula of royal adoption, and even if we are unable to disregard other meanings it has acquired over the centuries — we must realize once again that the literal meaning of the expression in 2 Sam. 7 is a statement about human relationships. It encompasses all conceivable aspects of relationships between father and son, not only with regard to duties and obligations, but emotional as well. Proof of this can be found in the second part of the verse (2 Sam. 7:14b) from which it becomes clear that the

71. Weinfeld, "Covenant" (1970) sees the continuation of the adoption formula in the phrase "ask of me" (Ps. 2:8) as originating in the promise of Land, or any other promise made by an overlord to his loyal vassal.
On kings in the ancient Near East who were called sons of the gods, including reference to the Egyptian adoption formula, see McCarter, *II Samuel* (1984), p. 207. However, he has reservations about the conclusions generally drawn from the Egyptian examples. In Egypt, it was believed that the king was a physical offspring of his divine father. So the Egyptian concept has no direct relevance to the biblical literature.
72. Smith, *Samuel* (1899), p. 302.
73. Japhet, *Chronicles H* (1977), pp. 349, 390; *Chronicles ET* (1989), pp. 411–412, 463–464.

father-son relationship also implies that when the son has done wrong, God will reprimand him in a way acceptable to man. If this interpretation is correct the divine reactions will necessarily be very different from the outbursts of wrath known heretofore.[74] Such an interpretation fits the concept prevalent in the Bible, in which adoption is understood in a symbolic, not a mythological sense. Nevertheless, it is no coincidence that in this particular context there is an echo of a Royal adoption formula. In phrasing the Divine promise of the eternal kingdom, the author uses language suggestive of great and glorious kingdoms.[75]

74. McCarter, *II Samuel* (1984), p. 407.
Eichrodt, *Theologie* (1948), vol. 1 pp. 6–39; *Theology* (1961) vol. 1 pp. 36–39 believes that only at this historical stage was the ground laid for a permanent system of relationships, expressed in a covenant and relieved of the fear of arbitrariness.
It is worth adding that this verse does not speak of, or even hint at, the possibility that royal sins may bring punishment upon the people, an idea that is quite important in Deuteronomistic historiography. When the king sins, the people are punished, and when the king falls, so do the people. The lack of a statement to that effect in this prophecy may support the argument that we are not dealing here with a Deuteronomistic redaction. See Lohfink, "Individum" (1960).
But from this standpoint, too, we witness a significant change with regard to the responsibility for sin. McCarthy, "Wrath" (1974), points out that this prophecy represents a turning point: heretofore the prophets spoke to the people and considered them the guilty ones (see Jud. 6:7–10). But from now on, the criticism and the wrath are directed at the king.
75. Von Rad, "Königsritual" (1947); "Royal Ritual" (1966), believes that in Israel, the idea of adoption carried no mythological connotation, as in ancient Egypt, but was understood in a symbolic, rather than a physical sense. Nevertheless, he argues that as far back as the time of David, the foundations were laid for absorbing elements from Egyptian literature and from the realities of the Egyptian monarchy. He points to similarities between the Egyptian 'royal novella' and the biblical narratives. See Morenz, "Königsliteratur" (1954).
On the similarities with Egypt in the titles given in the Bible to kings, as they ascend the throne, see von Rad, *Theologie* (1958), vol. 1 pp. 333–334; *Theology* (1962), vol. 1 pp. 335–336.
It is also worthy of note that in the opinion of von Rad, "Königspsalmen" (1940), the royal hymns in the Book of Psalms are directed to the idealized

From the beginning of the description of these relationships — "when your days are fulfilled" (vs. 12), which is a declaration of a promise for the future — we learn that it is contrary to, or at least substantially different from the existing relationship between God and his king. From what has been said until now, it can be surmised that close relationships between father and son, God and king, are dependent on the establishment of a royal dynasty, and had not before existed.[76]

On the other hand, however, the stability and perpetuation of the dynasty are dependent on these relations, since after describing them the author again declares: "And your house and your kingdom shall be made sure forever before thee; your throne shall be

concept of the king as God's anointed one, rather than to his historical appearance.

Noth, "Gott, König, Volk" (1950); "God, King and Nation" (1966), also argues that it is doubtful whether in the process of settling the Land of Israel, the Canaanite concept of the relations between the deity and the king was absorbed. Basing himself on Euler, "Königtum" (1938), he states that among the Arameans, for example, there is no mention of the divine descent of the king or of his deification. On the contrary, the king is presented primarily as the servant of the people.

There are assumptions that the linguistic formulation testifies to a personal father-son relationship without any sign of a tradition of adoption. See Brin, "Formula" (1972).

Some scholars think that 2 Sam. 7 reflects the festive ceremony of coronation that took place during the Feast of Tabernacles. The drama consisted of an assembly, a parade and a royal sacrifice in the temple, as well as a recitation of the covenant between the Lord and the House of David, and the choice of Mount Zion as the Divine residence. For a survey, see Kraus, *Königshaft* (1951). Eichrodt, *Theologie* (1948), pp. 94–95; *Theology* (1961), pp. 123–124 however, rejects this view. He argues that a literary analysis shows that there is no basis whatever for the claim that a recitation of the covenant with David was part of the ceremony. Also see McCarter, *II Samuel* (1984), p. 207.

76. On the connection between bringing up the Ark and the promise of a dynasty, as part of the changes of concept following the transition from the tradition of the Ark to the tradition of Zion, see Gese, "Davidsbund" (1964); Richter, "Nagid" (1965); Jeremias, "Lade" (1971).

established for ever" (vs. 16).[77] Therefore one should not consider vs. 16 as merely a repetition of vs. 13, but as part of a sophisticated structure. In other words, we are given to understand that a stable, permanent dynasty provides a literary framework and an ideological background for the functioning of the deity, who is now perceived differently from before.[78] From now on the Lord will be acting according to the standards of easily understood human morality. God's relationship with the ruler will be one of close intimacy,[79] bestowed permanently and will never again be denied.

A study of some aspects of the prayer of David may reinforce the conclusion that the dependence is mutual.

Nathan's Prophecy (2 Sam. 7:1–17) and David's Prayer (2 Sam. 7:18–29)

A cursory view of the texts (see table on p. 105), seems to show that the key expressions in Nathan's prophecy are almost identically distributed in David's prayer. The prayer is basically an expression of thanks for God's promise. At the same time, both its content, stressing as it does certain details, and the carefully balanced choice of words, are likely to create the impression that the prayer contains, in addition to thanksgiving, David's 'confirmation' or 'consent'. He emphasizes "Therefore thou art great, O Lord God" (vs. 22) and "confirm for ever the word which thou hast spoken... and do as thou hast spoken" (vs. 25) — something which

77. On the continuation of David's dynasty being contingent upon keeping all the commandments, as in 1 Kings 2:3–4; 8:25; 9:5–6 — see Šanda, *Könige* (1911); Weinfeld, "Covenant" (1970).

78. According to Alt, "Königtum" (1951); "Monarchy" (1968), the theological basis of the regime from now on (i.e., from the consolidation of the kingdom in Judah), is to be found in the idea of the "eternal covenant", rather than in the charismatic concept. (See also 2 Sam. 23:5; Jer. 32:40, Ps. 89:4–5, 29; cf. Is. 55:3 and 2 Chr. 6:42).

79. It is now clear that in his relations with the Deity, the ruler represents the people over whom he is charged to rule by justice and righteousness. See Weinfeld, "Covenant" (1970).

is repeated in the final request (vs. 29). True, this chapter does not speak explicitly in terms of covenant,[80] but since the content reflects an obligation, it is worth noting that the mutuality is restricted to one fairly well-defined point: God will magnify David and his name, and David will magnify God's name. This being so, the position of the word "magnify" in the text is apparently of significance. As already noted the second half of vs. 9 reflects a transition of the past to the future. It promises David: "...a great name, like the name of the great ones of the earth". This expression is constantly echoed in David's prayer, as if hinting that this is its most important point: "all this greatness" (vs. 21), and "therefore thou art great" (vs. 22); and, when God fulfils his promise of "thy name will be magnified for ever" (vs. 26). That is to say in this context God's greatness is a result of His having made David "great", whether we accept a specific interpretation for this expression, viz. David will be the heir of those who have been known as "great", or whether the expression is understood in its general accepted sense.[81]

Verse 26

Furthermore, an analysis of the structure of vs. 26 shows it to be a concise expression of the idea of mutual warranty: God's name will be great, and the writer continues "saying", "The Lord of hosts is God over Israel",[82] and "the house of thy servant David will be

80. The terms of the covenant appear clearly in the psalms that relate to this text: Ps. 89 & 132. See also von Rad, *Theologie* (1958), vol. 1 p. 309; *Theology* (1962), vol. 1 p. 311. Also, see above notes 59 and 61.

81. Von Rad, "Königsritual" (1947); "Royal Ritual" (1966), finds here royal attributes, as in Is. 9:5, or in 1 Kings 1:47. McCarter, *II Samuel* (1984), p. 201, points out that the expression is common to all ancient Near Eastern languages, as a title of the aristocracy, and compares the text with 2 Sam. 3:38.

82. On the term ה' צבאות (God of Hosts), especially in relation to גדולה (greatness) and עד עולם (for ever), see Strikowsky, "Lord of Hosts" (1972); Ross, "Yahweh Sebaoth" (1976).

established before thee", i.e., his interpretation is that the Lord's greatness has these two aspects. Furthermore, it is selfevident that the stability of the House of David having been 'established' is also a consequence of the Lord's being "God over Israel".

Moreover, we must pay attention to the fact that, apart from the declaration about the magnification of God's name, which will result from keeping his promise to David, the prayer contains no obligation on David's part.[83] Yet, perhaps we ought to understand the expression "and thy name will be magnified for ever" to be not only a promise of gratitude, i.e., not only a recompense God will receive for keeping his word, but also an element of prayer (is this a conventional feature?): in many supplicatory prayers this phrase, or one with similar meaning, ("for God's name", etc.) is used constantly.[84] In many prayers — a phrase of this kind is used as a final plea to strengthen the request.[85]

This, together with what we have said about the parallel distribution of keywords in Nathan's prophecy and David's prayer, may add weight to the assumption that this entire chapter is not only an 'ideological programme' but also a polemic.

Here too, as in the story of bringing up the Ark, the polemical character is emphasized by the explicit contrast between the House

83. A comparison with Genesis 15 strengthens the supposition that 2 Sam. 7 may be a report on the situation of making of a contract, rather than a prayer. See Clements, *David* (1967), p. 54.
84. McCarthy, "Deuteronomistic History" (1965), claims that David's prayer is based on an ancient ritual. He cites an example of a prayer of Sargon that contains similar elements. He also thinks that the formula כי אתה... דברת... (for you... have spoken) may be the end of the rite of bringing up the Ark. If so, this would be the conclusion of the blessing with which David intended to bless his House, which was written at the time of Solomon, who wished to attach the report on Nathan's prophecy to the older document on the bringing up of the Ark. See also Greenberg, "Prayers" (1982).
85. 1 Kings 8:41; 2 Chron. 6:32; Ps. 106:8; and especially Jer. 10:7; as well as Ps. 6:5; 23:3; 25:11 (7); 31:4; 44:27; 48:12; 79:9; 143:11.

of David and the House of Saul: "but I shall not depart my steadfast love from him, as I took it from Saul, whom I put away from before you" (vs. 15). There is no mention of Saul in the parallel passage in Chronicles (1 Chr. 17:13) or in the Septuagint. Some maintain that 2 Sam. 7:15 is the result of extensive editing.[86] It seems to me, however, that we must not ignore the consistency of the references to the House of Saul in the texts under consideration. Furthermore, even if Saul is not mentioned by name, the Chronicles text clearly indicates him: "from him who was before you" (1 Chr. 17:13). The triple use of the Hebrew root סו"ר (depart, remove, withdraw) emphasizes the message: the withdrawal of grace was connected with the removal of David's predecessor. This being so, the change David has brought about is what guarantees the eternal grace of God.[87] God's previous behaviour resulted from conditions and circumstances that have been removed.[88]

An argument such as this was probably devised to defend and justify the change, and to allay fears. It therefore seems to me that most of the chapter, except from some isolated additions,[89] is a contemporary composition that sums up Davids deeds and sees them as a theological revolution. Does this mean that the story was composed towards the end of David's reign, or perhaps even in Solomon's time, after the Temple was already built?

86. Smith, *Samuel* (1899), pp. 301–302, is of the opinion that in Chronicles (LXX and MT) we find three stages of the formation of the text. For more on the problem of this text and its history, see Abramsky, *Kingdom* (1977), p. 241 note 62.

87. It is difficult for me to accept the opinion of Rost, *Thronnachfolge* (1926), pp. *Succession* (1982), pp. 48–49, who believes that these words conceal a criticism of Ephraim, written after the exile of the Northern Kingdom in 722 B.C.

88. Abramski, *Kingdom* (1977), pp. 209–210.

89. Perhaps only vs. 13a and the final version of vss. 7 & 11 can be considered additions; but I am in no position to make a judgment on this point.

The Scheme of 2 Sam. 7

1.	ישב בביתו						
2.	יושב בבית						
	ישב בתוך	היריעה					
5.	תבנה לי בית לשבתי						
6.	כי לא ישבתי בבית	מתהלך באהל ומשכן					
7.		בכל אשר התהלכתי	לרעות				
	למה לא בניתם						
	לי בית ארזים						
8.			מאחר הצאן				
			נגיד				
9.		בכל אשר הלכת		שם גדול			
				כשם הגדולים			
10.					ונטעתיו		
					ושכן		
					והניחותי		
11.	בית יעשה לך ה׳						
12.						והכינותי	
						את	
						ממלכתו	
13.	הוא יבנה בית לשמי					וכננתי	
						את כסא	
						ממלכתו	עד עולם

16.ונאמן ביתך				וממלכתך	עד עולם
				כסאך	
				נכון	עד עולם
18.ומי ביתי					
19.בית עבדך					
21.		את כל			
		הגדולה הזאת			
22.		על כן גדלת			
23.	אשר הלכו	ולעשות לכם			
		הגדולה			
24.				ותכונן	עד עולם
25.על עבדך ועל					
ביתו			הקם		עד עולם
26.ובית עבדך		ויגדל (שמך)		נכון	עד עולם
27.בית אבנה לך					
29.וברך את בית					
עבדך					לעולם
ומברכתך					
יברך בית עבדך					לעולם

1. ...dwelt in his house...
2. ...dwell in a house...
...dwells in a tent...
5. ...build me a house to dwell in...
6. ...I have not dwelt in a house ... moving about in a tent for my dwelling...
7. ...in all places where I have moved ...to shepherd...why have you not built me a house of cedar...
8. ...from following the sheep...prince over my people...
9. ...a great name... of the great ones...
10. ...will plant...may dwell...disturbed no more...
11. ...the Lord will make you a house...
12. ...I will establish his kingdom...
13. ...he shall build a house for my name, and I will establish the throne of his kingdom for ever...
16. ...and your house and your kingdom shall be made sure for ever...your throne shall be established for ever...
18. ...what is my house...
19. ...thy servant's house...
21. ...all this greatness ...
22. ...therefore thou are great...
23. ...whom God went to...and doing for them great..
24. ...and thou didst establish... for ever...
25. ...confirm for ever... concerning thy servant and concerning his house...
26. ...(and thy name) will be magnified for ever... and the house of thy servant... will be established...
27. ...I will build you a house...
29. ...to bless the house of thy servant... for ever... and with thy blessing shall the house of thy servant be blessed for ever.

(2 Sam. 7:1–29)

The above table illustrates several facts:

a) The word appearing most frequently in the chapter is בית (house), especially in combinations: ישב בבית (dwell in a house), בנה בית (build a house).[90] This is only natural, since the construction of the house is the subject of the chapter. Even though the use of a *Leitwort* (or keyword) is fairly common in biblical narratives, it nevertheless appears in only a minority of them. In the narratives where it does appear, it is generally not as frequent as in 2 Sam. 7.[91]

b) The entire chapter is built around, or based upon a system of roots and phrases that keep appearing: the roots הלך־התהלך (go, walk), והכינותי, וכננתי, נכון, ותכונן – כו"ן (establish, confirm), גדול, גדולים, גדולה, גדלת, ויגדל – גד"ל (great, magnify), כסא – ממלכה (throne – kingdom), עד עולם – לעולם (for ever, eternity). As has been said above, some expressions are related to "moving about": לרעות (sheperding), מאחר הצאן (from following the sheep), נגיד (prince); but many more are related to permanence: ונטעתיו (plant), ושכן (dwell), הניח – והניחותי (rest), הקם (establish), עד עולם (for ever). These words contribute to the feeling of confrontation between two worlds, or, at least, two opposing situations.

c) These expressions are distributed almost symetrically in the chapter. The two parts of the chapter are of almost identical length. The first part consists of seventeen verses, among them two introductory verses and an introduction to Nathan's prophecy (vs. 4) and a concluding verse (vs. 17). Nathan's speech itself comprises twelve verses. The second part, David's prayer, also contains twelve verses, but only about one-half of vs. 18 is an

90. McCarter, *II Samuel* (1984) p. 195 notes that בית (house) is the key word to the whole story, and he believes that, by means of the opening sentence, it ties in with 2 Sam. 6:20: "And David returned to bless his household".
For another attempt to connect this chapter with the account of bringing up the Ark, see above, note 84.
91. Buber, "Sprache" (1964), and especially "Leitwortstil" (1964).

introduction. One can therefore speak of two virtually equal parts, in which the various expressions are almost evenly distributed. Since the expressions that have been so divided are the key words to the central ideas, one may say that the structure of the chapter reflects a sensitivity to the balance of its contents. This structure intensifies the underlying feeling of tension between the two concepts (i.e., permanence and impermanence).

d) The same expressions appear as *Leitwort* in the verses that are generally considered to be later additions,[92] and there, too, they are distributed fairly symmetrically among verses that are considered as basically belonging to different layers.[93]

The above may well reinforce my assumption that the message of Nathan's prophecy and David's prayer was understood in almost identical fashion throughout the various permutations of the text on its way to final crystallization.

92. See above notes 34 & 37.
93. See above pp. 84–85 & note 35.

CHAPTER FIVE

THE STRUCTURE AND INTENTION OF 2 SAMUEL 5

The theological message of 2 Sam. 5 is expressed not so much in the reports the chapter contains, as in the way they are put together, which directly serves the religious ideology connected with the establishment of the kingdom of David.

A major difficulty in this chapter is the way it deals with the main events it describes: the conquest of Jerusalem and the victories over the Philistines. There have been many attempts to reconstruct these events, but it is doubtful whether there can ever be any consensus on the matter.

The chapter consists of a collection of reports with no apparent central subject. One gets the impression that the reports, because of their brevity and the rapidity with which they followed one another,[1] are illustrations of one topic, and we must try to find what that topic is.

The medieval commentators do not concern themselves with questions of unity and structure. Modern scholars deal mainly with

1. The notion that accounts of events may be a collection of illustrations of one specific idea finds confirmation in 2 Sam. 4. The connection between the story of Mephibosheth and the murder of Ish-bosheth, as well as the fragmented way the material is constructed, may clarify the author's intention to illustrate a general, widely accepted idea i.e., how the house of Saul was destroyed. Rashi offers an explanation: "He goes to recount how the kingship was taken away from the house of Saul." Likewise Kimhi. For more about this principle, see Cassuto, "Sequence" (1973).

two types of problem: the order of events and reports, and the literary unity of the various parts of the text.

Verses 1–3 report the anointing of David as king of all Israel. Vss. 4–5 are probably parts of a royal chronicle. Vss. 6–16 relate the capture of Jerusalem and the reign of David, and vss.17–25 describe the wars with the Philistines.

However, it is customary to point out the discrepancy between vss. 1–2, which speak of the "tribes of Israel", and vs. 3 that speaks of the "elders of Israel". It is generally accepted that the reports came from two different sources and were combined by an editor-author.[2] Likewise vs. 17 which tells about the Philistines' attempt to capture David, is regarded as being directly connected with vs. 3.[3] It is the editor-author who made that connection, by means of vs. 17, between the Philistine wars and the anointing of David.[4]

From the historical standpoint the sequence of events is usually seen differently from what is reported here. It is now generally accepted that the battle with the Philistines occured immediately after David was crowned,[5] and that Jerusalem was captured only after they were defeated. As to the uniting of the people of Israel, as described in vss. 1–3, this became possible only after the final defeat of the Philistines. Grønbaek (see above note 2) argues that if vss. 17–25 reporting the victories, were originally connected to vss. 1–3, we should have to ask why the Deuteronomist editor-author changed the order. Grønbaek's theory is that the editor-author may have wanted the account of the capture of Jerusalem to come first, because he regarded it as the most important feature. In this

2. Wellhausen, *Composition* (1889), p. 256. For an up-to-date survey on the question of the identity of the redactor, see Grønbaek, *Aufstieg* (1971), p. 148 note 87.
3. Noth, *Studien* (1943), p. 63.
4. Hertzberg, *Samuelbücher* (1960), p. 224; *Samuel* (1964), p. 270.
5. Budde, *Samuelbücher* (1902), pp. 218–226; *Samuel* (1894), pp. 78–79, 81.

way he presents the Philistines' campaign as a reaction to the capture of Jerusalem rather than to the anointing of David.[6]

Viewing 2 Sam. 5 as the climax and conclusion of the story of David's ascent to the throne, Grønbaek claims that it is impossible to consider vss. 17–25 as the concluding ones: they are inappropriate in their present position. It would make much better sense if the culmination were the capture of Jerusalem.

Hertzberg, on the other hand, sees vss. 1–12 as a single unit albeit a unit composed of four parts. In his opinion, the information conveyed in this chapter is a direct result of the assassination of Ishbosheth (2 Sam. 4), and therefore no editorial changes were made in the order of events.

The account of the establishment of the house of David in Jerusalem and the Philistine wars (vss. 13 ff.) have also been subjected to various interpretations. It is often claimed that they are not in the right place: if the capture of Jerusalem was possible only after the defeat of the Philistines, then the list of children born to David in Jerusalem appears too early. Furthermore, the report of the relations established with King Hiram of Tyre (vs. 11), is in the wrong place, since it is unlikely that David would allow so much attention to be drawn to himself, before overcoming the Philistines.[7] There are those who therefore assume that this particular piece of information may belong in 2 Sam. 8.[8] According to this view, vss. 13–16, containing the list of David's children, were added by the same hand that added the story of 'David's Ascent' to the 'Succession Narrative, whereas the summary of David's reign in Hebron and Jerusalem (vss. 4–5) was added by the Deuteronomist.[9]

6. Liver, "Anointing" (1968).
7. Noth *Studien* (1943), p. 63; Ward, David's Rise (1967), pp. 167–170.
8. Noth, *Geschichte* (1950), p. 196 note 2; *History* (1958), p. 178 note 2.
9. Hertzberg, *Samuelbücher* (1960), p. 271; *Samuel* (1964), pp. 329–330. Mett-

Another approach, a literary-ideological one, is that of Abramski.[10] In his view, the focus of the chapter is on Jerusalem — as the central element in the royal ideology that characterizes the stories of David's reign. For this reason the list contains the names only of the children born to David **in Jerusalem**, in contrast to the list of his children born in Hebron (2 Sam. 3:2–5). The Jerusalem list is clearly preferred to the other, and is given greater prominence. The inclusion of Solomon's name is a hint that one of the sons born in Jerusalem will be David's successor. Similarly, the passage about Hiram and David's relations with him is tied in with the main theme, which is the strengthening of Jerusalem. However, when seeking the reason for the chapter being arranged as it is, on the whole I prefer the approach that looks for an ideological common denominator. I find it difficult to agree with the view that Jerusalem is the unifying factor, or the main theme of the whole chapter. An analysis of the design and structure of the chapter may help us to determine what is the common denominator.

General Characteristics

Even though the main accounts are in direct speech, or include direct speech, they are not constructed as dramatic occurences.

> The tribes of Israel say to David: "Behold, we are your bone and flesh. In times past, when Saul was king over us, it was you that led out and brought in Israel; and the Lord said to you, 'You shall be shepherd of my people Israel, and you shall be prince over Israel'" (vss. 1–2). The Jebusites say to David: "You will not come in here, but the blind and the lame will ward you off" (vs. 6). David's query to God: "Shall I go up against the Philistines? Wilt thou give them into my hand?". God's reply: "Go up; for I will certainly

inger, *King & Messiah* (1976), p. 115 esp. note 18 maintains that vs. 3 preserves the true tradition of the coronation.

10. Abramski, "Historiography" (1977).

give the Philistines into your hand" (vs. 19). God's reply to David in the valley of Rephaim: "You shall not go up; go around to their rear, and come upon them opposite the balsam trees. And when you hear the sound of marching in the top of the balsam trees, then bestir yourself; for then the Lord has gone out before you to smite the army of the Philistines" (vss. 23–24).

It is easy to see that the direct speech is an independant element, intended to illustrate the essence of the event, rather than a drawn-out description of the scene. Not even one event is presented as a dramatic scene or as a real happening is usually reported (such as the dramatic scenes in Genesis 12:13 ff.; 15 etc.). In 2 Sam. 5 every section only states the purpose and climax of the event, not its development. From this it can be inferred that there is no intention, in this collection of accounts, to tell the story of what actually happened. The intention is to point to something, whose accumulated details represent an argument or sample. If we succeed in identifying this 'something' we will understand the principle underlying the structure and its ideological message.

Detalied Analysis

Verses 1–3

"Then all the tribes of Israel came to David at Hebron, and said, 'Behold, we are your bone and flesh. In times past, when Saul was king over us, it was you that led out and brought in Israel; and the Lord said to you, 'You shall be shepherd of my people Israel, and you shall be prince over Israel.' So all the elders of Israel came to the King at Hebron; and king David made a covenant with them at Hebron before the Lord, and they anointed David king over Israel."

This declaration by "all the tribes of Israel" is not a realistic reconstruction of an event that took place on a particular occasion. There is certainly good reason to assert that we have here a truncated summary of two scenes. The main purpose of the declaration is to show that support of David is unconditional, and has three causes: a. The feeling of close relationship: "we are your bone and flesh";[11] b. Historical reasoning. Whether we understand the phrase המוציא והמביא (led out and brought in) in the narrow sense of command in war,[12] or regard it as a merismus, referring to all spheres of life, this part of the declaration is consonant with the tendency indicated in 2 Sam. 1:10 and 3:9–10: The crown and bracelet brought by the Amalekite, and Abner's statement that he knew what the Lord had sworn to David, indicate that 'public opinion' not only in Judah, but, surprisingly also in Israel and even outside it, recognized David as the candidate for the throne and such recognition was natural and obvious.[13]

It is appropriate to note here that all the literary devices are similar: they are all designed to penetrate the reader's consciousness indirectly. But in each case the speaker had a different purpose: the Amalekite brought the news of Saul's death (2 Sam. 1); Abner tells Ishbosheth angrily

11. Ward, David's Rise (1967) p. 169 argues that this declaration by the tribes of Israel is a response to David's great success in his war against the Philistines.
12. It is generally accepted that המוציא והמביא (the going out and coming in) refers to leadership in war. This is the case in 1 Sam. 29:6, 2 Sam. 3:25; 2 Kings 19:27 (Isaiah 37:28), Ps. 121:8 etc.
Nevertheless, it seems to me that in the light of the context, which represents David as the leader who is to become king over all of Israel, this expression may be regarded as merismus.
Smith, *Samuel* (1899), p. 286 maintains that the true meaning is 'actual leader.' So does Schulte, *Geschichtsschreibung* (1972), p. 135.
13. Budde, *Samuelbücher* (1902), p. 27; *Samuel* (1894), p. 55; Eissfeldt, *Komposition* (1931), p. 120. Following both, Ward, David's Rise (1967), p. 169, maintains that the argument that the Lord made a vow to David is well

that in future he will support David (2 Sam. 3); and finally, "all the tribes of Israel" come together to anoint David as king (2 Sam. 5:1). This way we learn quite incidentally from each speaker separately that everyone sees David as the true leader and natural successor to the throne. If we also bear in mind that the speakers were highly emotional, angry, or extremely solemn, they become more credible. The set up obscures the fact that it was the author who put the lines into their mouths, making it appear that they were moved by sincere emotion. We have here a very sophisticated literary ruse.

c. The author uses 'public opinion' as a rhetorical device,[14] but we now note that the third cause for supporting David is that the words came from the Lord.

There may be a significant difference between the intention of making David a נגיד (prince) (vs. 2) and anointing him as king (vs. 3).[15] It may be that this difference also reflects the tension pointed out in earlier chapters. It is possible that the phrase "the tribes of Israel" represents the tribal desire that the ruler, as נגיד (prince) should guarantee the continuation of their tradition. What was said later testifies to the fact that the highest tribal body, namely the "elders of Israel", had confirmed the institution of kingship.[16]

grounded: when David enquired of the Lord at Nob he was told that he would become king; but in the story of Nob (1 Sam. 21) this promise was omitted.

14. For examples of exploiting public opinion, whether real or imaginary, as a rhetorical element in literature, and the influence of similar literary devices, see Perry, "Literary Dynamics" (1979).
15. Hertzberg, *Samuelbücher* (1960), p. 270; *Samuel* (1964), pp. 328–329. In his opinion, this passage reflects a two-phase negotiation. The two phases are manifested in the words נגיד (captain) in vs. 2 and מלך (king) in vs. 3. The latter can be seen almost as a second scene.
16. Alt, *Staatenbildung* (1930).

Even if originally vss. 1–2 & vs. 3 came from two different sources (see above note 2), the combined text creates a continuity in the development of the approach to the monarchy.

Furhtermore, even if originally there was a significant difference between נגיד (crown-prince, ruler) and מלך (king), the present combined text treats the two as roughly the same.

The portion of the declaration that emphasizes the Lord's part in the unfolding events, is the binding factor of the chapter. It turns out, particularly in the light of previous chapters, that David did not win the Kingship, merely on account of his actions, intrigues or characteristics. On the contrary, 2 Sam. 3 quite clarifies that there was a surprising disparity between his actions and their consequences. It requires only a slight stretch of the imagination to realize that everything was directed by the Lord. **But the author does not present this awareness in so many words. The story is so constructed as to make it clear that it was David himself who had this theological insight**. Indeed, this is how the author of 2 Sam. 5 will go on presenting things. Therefore, when there is 'feedback' on the subject from the people, it is obvious that they were in theological accord with the king.[17]

Verses 4–5

> "David was thirty years old when he began to reign, and he reigned forty years. At Hebron he reigned over Judah seven years and six months; and at Jerusalem he reigned over all Israel and Judah thirty three years."

I shall deal later with the inclusion of chronical material (pp. 127–128), as well as with the list in vss. 13–16. It is generally

17. Clements, *David* (1967), pp. 50–52. The two independent political entities, Judah and Israel, united of their own free will. There is a theory that this union centered on the personalitiy of the leader, without involving institutions of the

accepted that these verses were added by the Deuteronomist, whose point of view and purpose are clear,[18] and therefore belong together with vs. 10a. As to the reasons why the lists were removed from their original context and put in this particular place, there are only partial answers.[19] Eissfeldt recognizes that lists are generally relevant to the context in which they appear,[20] and this may explain why the editor truncated them and included only those portions pertaining to the material under discussion. The lists add authenticity to the narrative, not only as chronical material. By placing "thirty years" of David's reign in Jerusalem next to the declaration by the tribes of Israel, the author indirectly provides evidence that the declaration is not his own invention. In other words, we are made to understand that David did indeed establish his kingdom in Jerusalem, and reigned for thirty-three years. This summary statement serves a double purpose: a) It bridges two periods, of which the first serves as preparation and training for the second, more important one. b) From a literary aspect it covers the routine, everday happenings between the great famous episodes. This particular form of presentation was required here to provide balance, especially since in such a chapter the events do not appear as a detailed story, but rather as mere allusions or illustrations.

separate entities; i.e., that it was a personal union, so Alt, *Staatenbildung* (1930). However, this view has recently met with a great deal of criticism.

18. Flanagan, Traditions (1970), pp. 48, 90; Grønbaek, *Aufstieg* (1971), p. 248.
19. See Mazar, "Philistines" (1971), pp. 234–243. There is a hypothesis that after the murder of Ish-bosheth, David was king over Hebron for another five-and-a-half years. He had to wait so long because he feared the Philistines' reaction, as he was still their vassal. He needed an extended period to improve the quality of his army, and it was only when this was accomplished that he decided the time was ripe for the unification of the kingdom and the struggle with the Philistines. Garsiel, *David* (1975), pp. 20–21.
20. Eissfeldt, *Einleitung* (1956), pp. 31–33; 357–376; *Introduction* (1965), pp. 24–26; 268–281.

Verses 6–8 (9)

> "And the king and his men went to Jerusalem against the Jebusites, the inhabitants of the land, who said to David, 'You will not come in here, but the blind and the lame will ward you off — thinking, 'David cannot come in here.' Nevertheless David took the stronghold of Zion, that is, the city of David. And David said on that day, 'Whoever would smite the Jebusites, let him get up the water shaft to attack the lame and the blind, who are hated by David's soul.' Therefore it is said, 'The blind and the lame shall not come into the house.'"

I have already noted that many scholars consider this chapter the high point of the story of David's ascent to the throne, because it tells about the conquest of Jerusalem. However, this passage, even if supplemented by some other version, (e.g., 1 Chr. 11:4), does not really contain a clear description of that conquest.

The following is a summary of the main approaches to the subject: Josef Kara[21] surmised that the lame and the blind were "figures looking like human beings which Abraham made witness his pact with the Philistines that his progeny would not inherit this mountain, that as long as these figures were produced his progeny would not be allowed to drive the Jebusites out of Jerusalem. And when David appeared... they brought out these figures and said to him... as long as these figures are in our hands, you are not permitted to attack us on account of the oath that your forefather made."

This is an interesting idea, especially in view of its similarity to the explanation in modern research, in which "the blind and the lame" are interpreted as statues or puppets that play a part in the

21. Joseph Kara, in his interpretation of the expression העורים והפסחים (the blind and the lame), following *Pirkei de Rabbi Eliezer* 80:36 and *Yalkut Yehoshua* 247:28.

magic ceremonials involved in treaty-making. For example those containing the Aramaic אֵיךְ זִי, meaning "just as" in the Sephira contracts,[22] i.e., they would bring in wax dolls and destroy them saying: "Just as this wax burned by fire, so may Arpad be burned... just as this wax is burned by fire, so may M'atiel'...".[23]

Carlson explains the phrase "the lame and the blind" not in relation to magic rituals, but as an allusion to Jebusite personalities, similar to the story of Balaam (Num. 24:3, 15).[24]

Other scholars are of the opinion that "the lame and the blind" is intended to be understood literally: the Jebusites placed blind and lame on the wall, either as an expression of their contempt for the attackers, as if to say that even the blind and the lame could repel the attack,[25] or perhaps somebody within the walls (a collaborator?) was trying to hint to David, that it was not via the wall that Jerusalem could be taken,[26] i.e., the emphasis in the sentence is on לא... הנה (not... here).

These explanations give different meaning to the phrase "the water shaft",[27], and raise the question of Joab's role in the whole

22. Yadin, "Blind & Lame" (1952).
23. From Fitzmyer, *Inscriptions* (1967), pp. 14–15.
24. Carlson, *David* (1964), p. 52.
25. Stoebe, "Jerusalem" (1957), and following him Ward, David's Rise (1967), believe that the defenders actually placed their blind and their lame on top of the defence wall; the intention may have been to ridicule those who had failed to break into the fortress of Zion for lack of daring and imagination.
26. Dinur, "Jerusalem" (1946) believes that the meaning of the verse is: you will not enter here until you have removed the blind and the lame. According to him, the words were intended as a hint that it was easy to capture the city, as if to say: you will not get here, if those you have brought are blind and lame; while the interpretation that says: you will not enter because even the blind and the lame are against you, is based on the inaccurate translation by LXX, which reads ἀντέστησαν in an effort to circumvent the difficulty of the text.
27. On the צינור (water-shaft) as the source of the city's water, see Kenyon, *Royal*

affair, noting and trying to account for the fact that his name is not even mentioned in the report of 2 Sam. 5.[28]

The placing of the event in the overall chronological order (not only in 2 Sam. 5, but in the broader context) is also explained in various ways. Reviv reasons that the capture of Jerusalem must have taken place in the early years of David's reign in Hebron, since at the time of the wars against Abner and Ish-bosheth, Joab was already in command of David's men (2 Sam. 3:22), a position he was given as a kind of reward for the conquest of Jerusalem. Moreover, the route north of Hebron was already open at this stage, and the Jerusalem fortress was already in David's hands.[29]

A novel attempt to reconstruct the capture of Jerusalem, while relying on the main approaches mentioned here,[30] makes us realize

Cities (1971), p. 31. For various interpretations of the word as parts of the body, see Ward, David's Rise (1967), pp. 174, 179.
A very different and far-fetched emendation and interpretation was suggested by Tur Sinai, *Peschuto* (1964), who reads: את הכל מכה יבוס ומנגע בצנור meaning: Jebus (the city-god) hits everything, and smites with the צנור (= the weapon of the god of lightning and thunder).

28. Auerbach, *Wüste* (1938), vol. 1 pp. 217–221, thinks that storming the city was a trick by David to get rid of Joab, who he had never forgiven for the murder of Abner. He tries to reconstruct the event assuming that MT of 2 Sam. 5 is incomplete, because the scribe when copying this verse misinterpreted the part about the blind and the lame. Auerbach thinks they were hated intensely by David, and that this is the source of the prohibition in Lev. 21:18. This misinterpretation somehow found its way from the margin into the text itself, replacing the original verse that was preserved in Chronicles. Only the words "let him get up the water-shaft" remained in 2 Sam. 5:8, but they were dropped by the Chronicler, because he did not know what they meant.
Razin, *Census* (1976), pp. 126–155 prefers the LXX version, among other things because of its closeness to 1 Chron. 11:4–6. Also, in his opinion the MT of 2 Sam. ignores the role of Joab in the conquest, because this account was included in the broad general summary of David's kingship.
29. See especially Mazar, "David's Reign" (1963), and also Reviv, *Clan* (1979), pp. 123–124.
30. Herzog-Gichon, *Battles* (1978), pp. 77–79. Their supposition is that David

even more sharply the extent to which we must fill the gaps by speculation. However, one should not ignore the way biblical narrative describes battles. Licht[31] has pointed out that generally, an event is so condensed, into a 'narrow scene': an entire battle may be represented by a confrontation between two men. Sometimes there is no description at all, and the news of the battle takes the form of a very brief summary. Thus, an important, even decisive battle such as that between Jephtah and the Ammonites, is not reported in detail, but mentioned in one verse only. In the passage Jud. 11:29–33, vs. 33 alone tells directly of the battle. Vs. 29 describes Jephtah's route to battle, vss. 30–31 his vow, whereas vs. 32 gives the result of the campaign in advance. We may conclude that the author is not interested in the actual fighting; his purpose is not to write a comprehensive history, but to focus on the hero of the story.

The author's major task is to present the situation and the character of the hero. The description of a battle, a war, or indeed any historical event, will only include such details as serve the writer's purpose. In other words, the whole picture is reduced to events on the individual plane.

This is accepted procedure in biblical narrative. It is therefore not at all surprising that a major event, or even a climactic event of an historic development is not described in detail. What is more surprising is the construction of a passage such a 2 Sam. 5:6–8: two distinct elements seem to have been combined here. There are scenic elements, such as direct speech and dialogue, side by side with chronical elements, summary statements, aetiological addi-

succeeded in capturing the fortress, but failed to enter the city itself. The enlistment of the blind and lame to help defend the city was intended as an act of magic. David noticed the tunnel that had been cut in the rock, leading down the eastern slope of the mountain range to the spring of Gihon. In a surprise attack, preceded by a diversionary action which caused the enemy to concentrate his attention on the northern sector, David caught the Jebusites off guard.

31. Licht, "Mimesis" (1976).

tions and midrashic name derivations. The scenic parts are fragmentary, not because there is no continuation to "whoever would smite the Jebusites, let him get up the water shaft" (vs. 8),[32] but because in neither vs. 6 nor vs. 8 is there any response to the challenge thrown out in the direct speech. It might well be expected that the full story, including a description of the tensions and the difficulties involved in capturing a city, would contain an exchange of challenges and responses. This is usual between those attacking and those defending a wall: see for instance Judges 8:5–7; 1 Kings 20:10–11).[33]

The chronical and aetiological elements are also intermingled. Thus for example, vss. 7 and 9 represent the chronical element,[34] whereas vs. 8b (and perhaps also parts of vs. 6) are aetiological.

This structure suggests that the author accumulated fragmentary information relating to the capture of Jerusalem only for use as allusions or illustrations (see above pp. 111–112), and not for the purpose of reconstructing the event in detail. It is reasonable to suppose that this fragmentation was partly due to the author's desire to omit any mention of Joab. It is therefore that one must consider the possibility, that the Septuagint (closely related to 1 Chr. 11:4–6) preserved the better text.

The Septuagint reads: ... Οὐκ εἰσελεύσει ὧδε, ὅτι ἀντέστησαν οἱ τυφλοὶ καὶ οἱ χωλοί, λέγοντες ὅτι Οὐκ εἰσελεύσεται Δαυιδ ὧδε ... καὶ εἶπεν Δαυιδ τῇ ἡμέρᾳ ἐκείνῃ Πᾶς τύπτωυ Ιεβουσαῖον ἁπτέσθω ἐν παραξιφίδι καὶ τοὺς χωλοὺς καὶ τοὺς τυφλοὺς καὶ τοὺς μισοῦντας

32. In the opinion of Tur Sinai, *Peschuto* (1964), p. 195, 2 Sam. 6:8 is incomplete. See above note 27.
33. On the structure of a conversation and of a scene, see Licht, *Storytelling* (1978), pp. 24–50.
34. The Millo is part of the fortress of Ofel (the strategically weak spot of the City of David on the northern side, vss. 9–11 include a description of some of the public buildings erected under David's rule. (בית ארזים = a house of cedar,

τὴν ψυχὴν Δαυιδ· διὰ τοῦτο ἐροῦσιν Τυφλοὶ καὶ χωλοὶ οὐκ εἰσελεύσονται εἰς οἶκον κυρίου. = ...Do not come in here because the blind and the lame have been removed (or: have arisen?) saying: for David shall not enter here... and David said: whoever strikes a Jebusite will touch with his spear the blind, the lame and all who hate David's soul. Therefore they say 'the blind and the lame shall not come into the house' (2 Sam. 5:6, 8).

Perhaps there really was a division of tasks between David and Joab, and the text before us, wishing to deal only with David, caused the truncating of the text. It is certain, however, that this was not the only reason the text was 'cut to pieces', thereby acquiring its present form.

I am in no position to add to these suggestions (see above note 33). From the many diverse views mentioned one may possibly arrive at the following conjecture: The truncated nature of the collection is most apparent in the second half of vs. 8 which may refer to a specific custom or tradition, well known when the text was originally written, but not by the time of its final redaction. Perhaps "the lame and the blind" were really involved in some magical ceremony, practiced by the Jebusites. In this case, it might be assumed that, since these rites and ceremonies were particularly abhorrent to David because of his difficulty in capturing Jerusalem, he set out to uproot them and anything connected with them. This may explain the order that they "shall not come into the house" (2 Sam. 5:8). Since the author had decided to present the capture of Jerusalem as an illustration of David's special relationship with the Lord, he finds it necessary to mention that from now on anything connected with magical rites is taboo. If so, this brief reference underscores the theological aspect of the capture of Jerusalem. Therefore the military aspect of the campaign was of no interest to the editor, who accordingly omits the name of Joab from the story.

mentioned in 2 Sam 7:2, belongs to the same set of buildings). See Aharoni, *Archaeology* (1982), pp. 192–194.

Verses 11–16

a. vss. 11–12

> "And Hiram king of Tyre sent messengers to David, and cedar trees, also carpenters and masons who built David a house. And David perceived that the Lord had established him king over Israel, and that he had exalted his kingdom for the sake of his people Israel."

The connection between this paragraph and the following list of sons could be the idea that close foreign relationships are a guarantee to a stable dynasty. Abramski, however, maintains that this paragraph was placed here because it is also connected with the accounts about the strengthening of Jerusalem's position. In his opinion Jerusalem and its status are the main subject of this chapter.[35]

The passage ends in a manner similar to the previous one: "And David perceived that the Lord had established him king of Israel, and that he exalted his kingdom for the sake of his people Israel." (2 Sam. 5:12). These theological statements were taken by scholars to be the work of editors. Grønbaek[36] maintains that vs. 10a was originally a continuation of vss. 4–5, and Schulte[37] argues that vss. 6–9 originally followed vss. 17–25. In her opinion, vs. 10 was originally in the nature of a summary of all the events in the chapter. Vs. 12 is generally taken to be a Deuteronomistic comment.[38]

It may well be that vss. 10 and 12 are two different formulations, derived from different sources, dealing with the same subject. In their present form we note that a clear development has taken place between vss. 10 and 12. Vs. 10 merely notes a fact: "And

35. Abramski, "Historiography" (1977).
36. Grønbaek, *Aufstieg* (1971), p. 248.
37. Schulte, *Geschichtsschreibung* (1972), p. 135.
38. Carlson, *David* (1964), p. 52 and note 2 there; see also McCarter, *II Samuel* (1984), pp. 144–146.

David became greater and greater, for the Lord, the God of Hosts, was with him"; whereas vs. 12 stresses: "And David perceived that the Lord had established him king over Israel, and that he exalted his kingdom for the sake of his people Israel." In other words, the development is in David's perception of what has happened. In the first statement (vs. 10) the Lord was with him, in the second (vs. 12), David recognizes this and understands that the Lord was acting not for his sake, but "for the sake of his people Israel." The events between these two stages represent two types of activity: internal reinforcement and fortification, and establishing foreign relations. Verses 10 and 12 therefore are tendentious links between the accumulated items. Unravelling the purpose of these connecting verses helps us to understand the principle behind the combinations in the entire chapter.

b. **Vss. 13–16**

> "And David took more concubines and wives from Jerusalem, after he came from Hebron, and more sons and daughters were born to David. And these are the names of those who were born to him in Jerusalem: Shammua, Shobab, Nathan, Solomon, Ibhar, Elishua, Nepheg, Japhia, Elishama, Eliada, and Eliphelet."

I have already noted that some scholars view this list as tendentious, intended to indicate Jerusalem's superiority over Hebron and hint at the future of the dynasty. Hertzberg maintains that the list originated in the royal archives, where the passages 3:2–5, 5:13–16 were part of one list (as they are in 1 Chr. 3:1–9). They were separated in order to differentiate what happened to David before he came to Jerusalem from what happened to him afterwards.[39] Dinur views the chapter as "the end of the story of David's rise to reign over all Israel," and maintains that the list comes at the end of the story, because this is the normal way of ending the story

39. Hertzberg, *Samuelbücher* (1960), pp. 221–222; *Samuel* (1964), p. 271.

of any ruler's successes. Hence he too argues that "when the Philistines heard..." etc., i.e., everthing reported in vss. 17–25, occurred earlier after the anointing, and is not in place after the list.[40] But Dinur does not explain the reason for the present arrangement.

Razin thinks that the distinction between the children born in Hebron and those born in Jerusalem is clear: the latter enjoyed special privileges. Furthermore, the purpose is to prepare the way for choosing Solomon as successor to the throne.[41]

The common view is that the material before us is a biased rewriting of the lists, although it is difficult to perceive where that tendentiousness lies. The only obvious thing is the existence of a dividing line: i.e., David is coming to Jerusalem. Further investigation, however, may clarify the reason for constructing the list (2 Sam. 5:13–16) in its present form.

Verses 17–25

> "When the Philistines heard that David had been anointed king over Israel, all the Philistines went up in search of David; but David heard of it and went down to the stronghold. Now the Philistines had come and spread out in the valley of Rephaim. And David inquired of the Lord, 'Shall I go up against the Philistines? Wilt thou give them into my hand?' And the Lord said to David, 'Go up; for I will certainly give the Philistines into your hand.' And David came to Baal-perazim, and David defeated them there; and he said, 'The Lord has broken through my enemies before me, like a bursting flood.' Therefore the name of the place is called Baal-perazim. And the Philistines left their idols there, and David and his men carried them away. And the Philistines came up yet again, and spread out in the valley of

40. See note 26 above.
41. Razin, *Census* (1976), p. 128.

> Rephaim. And when David inquired of the Lord, he said, 'You shall not go up; go around to their rear, and come upon them opposite the balsam trees. And when you hear the sound of marching in the tops of the balsam trees, then bestir yourself; for then the Lord has gone out before you to smite the army of the Philistines.' And David did as the Lord commanded him, and smote the Philistines from Geba to Gezer."

The report on the battles in the valley of Rephaim and in Baal-perazim is also fragmentary.[42]

Hertzberg believes that some material was cut, the deletion having occurred between המצודה (the stonghold), which he believes to be Adulam, and the report on the deployment of the Philistines.[43] The report is surprisingly brief. Comparing vs. 20 ("like a bursting flood") with 2 Sam. 23:12–17 and 21:15–22, he surmises that the original description of the event was more detailed and elaborate. Hertzberg believes that in the report of 2 Sam. 5, two episodes were combined for a reason that becomes clear in vs. 17. Grønbaek too[44] thinks that vss. 17–25, were once connected to vss. 1–3, i.e., that here we find the response to the expectation of great deeds, aroused by the anointing.[45]

42. Ward, David's Rise (1967), pp. 181–184 thinks that המצודה (the fortress) generally refers to the Zion fortress, but since it says here וירד (he went down), the reference must be to some desert fort. Thus two different stages seem to have become confused. He fails to see why vss. 17–25 were removed from their context, except insofar as they testify to the fulfilment of Abner's words in 2 Sam 3:18, and also round off a major subject in the story of David's rise. Vs. 25, he believes, comes from a secondary tradition.
43. Hertzberg, *Samuelbücher* (1960), pp. 223, 225; *Samuel* (1964), pp. 273–274 thinks that Adulam served as a military base for David's forays in the period preceding the Kingdom, according to 1 Sam. 22:1–5 (see also 2 Sam. 23:13 and 1 Chron. 11:15–16). The name Adulam may have been omitted from the end of vs. 17 in 2 Sam 5, due to a misunderstanding.
44. Grønbaek, *Aufstieg* (1971), p. 250.
45. Hertzberg, *Samuelbücher* (1960), p. 224; *Samuel* (1964), pp. 275–276; Grønbaek, *Aufstieg* (1971), p. 251.

Reviv assumes that the order of victories and conquests is not chronologically accurate. He believes that vss. 17–25 reflect a series of battles in which David beats the Philistines and drives them back as far as Gezer, subsequently defeating them on their own soil.[46] These battles therefore, belong to a later stage.

Carlson's approach is similar, He thinks the victory over the Philisitines was important for the bringing up the ark to Jerusalem, as described in 2 Sam. 6, because it was only this victory that opened the Gibeon-Gezer road, which according to Carlson was the route taken by David for the journey of the Ark. The theological aspect linking the two events is suggested in the phrase "then the Lord has gone out before you".[47]

An attempt to reconstruct the two battles with the Philistines, must necessarily be based on supposition and assumption. Here, as in the capture of Jerusalem, the only thing of which we can be certain is that advantage was taken of the topographical conditions to execute surprising stratagems. But the writer is certainly not interested in describing ruses that David could invent and execute himself. There can be no doubt that the writer's aim is to show what the Lord did to help David by direct intervention, making it look like a miracle (see above p. 115). It is possible that what we have here is merely a reference to an action that has been described in detail somewhere else, or was so well known that the writer found it unnecessary to describe it in full once again.[48]

The Midrash, as I have already indicated, tries to give the story an ideological slant: "Whenever the Philisitnes approached, the Israelites would see them: they were only four cubits away. So the Israelites said to David, 'Do we stand still?' And he said: 'I was

46. See also 2 Sam. 21:15–22 and Reviv, *Clan* (1979), pp. 124–125.
47. Carlson, *David* (1964), pp. 52–58.
48. See Weiss, "Law and Custom" pp. 13–14.

ordered from heaven to refrain from striking them until we see the treetops move to and fro...'. All at once all the trees began to move, and that attack began... And the Lord said to the angels: 'Look at the difference between David and Saul...'". The hint, of course, is to 1 Sam. 13, the battle of Michmash, where Saul did not wait for Samuel and proceeded on his own.[49]

This Midrash describes the condition of the terrain.[50] I do not share its view that the real purpose of the biblical description is to point out the difference between David and Saul in their obedience to the Lord's words. But here, too, we can learn of the writer's purpose from the frequency with which the Lord's name is mentioned and from his stress on the Lord's role in the victory.

As to the role of the aetiological explanation, I accept Seeligman's attitude, that in most instances the aetiological explanation is not the core of the story, nor is it its cause. Such explanations are often only marginal, and were secondary additions to existing stories.[51] We may therefore call a narrative aetiological, not because of the aetiological formula in it, but only when the aetiological problem in it, and the solution to it, themselves create the central tension and resolution which are necessary for any story. By this criterion, our story is not aetiological.[52] But even if we assume that the first part (vss. 17–21) once had an aetiological element, this has been blurred in the present form, since in the following section (vss. 22–25) there is no such aetiological

49. *Midrash Shoher Tov* Psalm 27 and *Pesikta Rabbati* 88. Also see above Introduction note 48.
50. It would seem that אז תצא במלחמה (then thou shalt go out to battle) of 1 Chron. 14:15, rather than אז תחרץ (then bestir yourself) of 2 Sam 5:24 is an attempt to smooth a difficulty.
51. Seeligmann, "Aetiology" (1961); "Erzählung" (1962); "Cultic Tradition" (1964). For examples of narratives that underwent later expansion by adding an aetiological layer, see Gen. 32:2b–3; 33:16–17.
52. For a survey of this subject see Wilcoxen, "Narrative" (1974), pp. 57–87.

formula.[53] For this reason we must continue the search for the rhetorical objective of the chapter.

The Common Denominator of the Various Elements of 2 Sam. 5.

In the light of what has been said, we can now examine the chapter for its overall meaning and try to pinpoint the purpose of combining the various episodes. The method employed will be twofold: an examination of 1) the dominant stylistic feature of the whole chapter; and 2) the common denominator in the different items of information. Then, after combining the two examinations, we shall be in a better position to reach the central message of the chapter.

1. The chapter uses no *Leitwort,* system of key words or combinations of expressions that might indicate its ideology. There is, however, conspicuous emphasis on the active presence, influence and decisive intervention of the Lord at every stage, and these manifestations are very carefully placed at — one is tempted to say distributed among — the crucial points in the chapter. They are as follows:

> 1. "And the **Lord** said to you, 'You shall be shepherd of **my** people Israel.'" (vs. 2)
> 2. "And David became great and greater, for the **Lord**, the **God of hosts**,[54] was with him." (vs. 10)
> 3. "And David perceived that the **Lord** had established him king over Israel, and that he had exalted **his** kingdom for the sake of his people Israel." (vs. 12)
> 4. "And David enquired of the **Lord**... And the **Lord** said to David: 'Go up...'." (vs. 19)

53. On this account see Kallai, "Baal-perazim" (1954).
54. On the name ה' צבאות see Strikowsky, "Lord of Hosts" (1972); Ross, "Yahweh Sebaoth" (1976).

5. "And he said, 'The **Lord** has broken through my enemies before me, like a bursting flood!'" (vs. 20, cf. Isa. 28:21)
6. "And when David inquired of the **Lord**, he said, 'You shall not go up; go around to their rear, and come upon them opposite the balsam trees. And when you hear... for then the **Lord** has gone out before you...'" (vss. 23–24)
7. "And David did as the **Lord** commanded him." (vs. 25)

One can say that these are the major elements uniting the various parts of the chapter and constituting its development as well as its ideological axis.

With regard to development, we note the following stages:

a. Recognition by the people that David has been called to his task by the Lord, whose word was being fulfilled.

b. The editor-author's attempt to ensure that the reader is aware of the connection between David's success and his close relationship with the Lord.

c. David's own awareness that it was the Lord who established his throne firmly; and the reason for His doing so.

d. David's actions, in the light of this awareness. From here on, the various stages (vss. 4–7) show the strengthening of the bond between the Lord and David. This bond is a result of an awareness that had gradually developed and crystallized.

The Common Denominator of the Content

I have just shown that the chapter contains something like a sample, or cross-section, of David's various types of activity. They are as follows: a) gaining the support of the people; b) consolidating the House of David (in two separate stages: first, in general; and second, consolidating and expanding his authority in Jerusalem; c) the capture of Jerusalem, and its transformation into the central site of power; d) establishing foreign relations; e) the defeat of the Philistines.

The above require some comment:

a) Support of the people: According to 2 Sam. 5:2 this was not the result of David's initiative. The people were aware that it was the Lord who told David, "You shall be shepherd of my people Israel."

b) Consolidation of the House of David: the concise chronicle of this information, left its mark on the entire chapter. Right after the account of the anointing, we are told on one hand, that "David was thirty years old when he began to reign" (5:4), and on the other, "and he reigned forty years" (5:4). If we take the chronicle vss. 4–5 as an introduction to what followed, then — because they cover the beginning and end of David's reign — the verse adds to the feeling that we are not following events chronologically, but summarizing it reflectively.

c–d) The tendentiousness in the choice of accounts now shows up very clearly. Had the editor-author considered the capture of Jerusalem as the climax of the story, it stands to reason that he would have paused here, to drive home the importance of the occasion. Then he would have painted a detailed scene by means of dialogue, speech or prayer. But this is not the case: this news is appended to the information about Hiram, which itself is placed between vs. 10 "and David became greater and greater, for the Lord, the God of hosts, was with him" and vs. 12: "and David perceived that the Lord had established him king over Israel, and that he had exalted his kingdom for the sake of his people Israel." Thus connecting the kingdom and its expansion. More than that, it clarifies the connection between David's deeds and the support of the Lord, especially David's awareness of it.

e) It is now possible to see that the main purpose of the account of the defeat of the Philistines is to stress the support and constant guidance David received from the Lord.

There can be no doubt that 2 Sam. 5:20 is not intended to be a description of the battle, for all it says about it is: And David defeated them there. In the same way "And when you hear the sound of marching in the tops of the balsam trees, then bestir yourself" (5:24) does not relate battle strategy. David's question, the detailed guidance he is given, the instructions and his obedience to them — all these accentuate the Lord's presence as the chief purpose of this account.

> The author's eagerness to tell what happened to the graven images belonging to the Philistines, may also be due to his attempt to present this as the Lord's reward to David — in literary anticipation — for bringing the Ark to Jerusalem. Perhaps there is also an intention to stress that just as the Ark had at one time fallen to the Philistines, as spoils of war, so their graven images have now fallen into the hands of David.[55]

Thus if we complete the paraphrasing so that we have a condensed summary of all the accounts, what remains will be something like the following: In all his succesful enterprises, in his relations with his people, in his stabilization of the dynasty, in his ruses, his foreign relations and his military victories, David recognized that it was the work of the Lord and that he had acted on the Lord's instructions.

This is even more apparent if we follow the sequence of events related in 2 Sam. 1–5. Through this sequence, one understands

55. See above note 49. The Babylonian Talmud states that they used to bring out the idols in victory parades, in an attempt to explain that there is no contradiction between 2 Sam 5:21 and 1 Chron. 14:12 (Babylonian Talmud, *Avodah Zarah* 54:1). See also Kimhi on וישאם (he carried them).

that the unexpected developments which culminated in the kingdom's falling into David's hand, led the people to the same conclusion.

The fact that the author prefers to present this basic idea through a series of truncated, disjointed descriptions, rather than through a final declarative statement (as is more typical of the Deuteronomistic style) is characteristic of the structure of 2 Sam. 1–8.

One should also point out that, despite their different approaches, scholars reach similar conclusions as to the aim of the book. The principle was already established by Hempel, who stated that the tie between the separate sagas and their incorporation within a complicated literary work was created to attain the desired conclusion, viz., that salvation never comes from human hands.[56] He thinks that the writer tries to convey an image of David as a man close to God.

It seems to me, however, that such conclusions require support by a meticulous study of the text, designed to elucidate the editor-author's literary devices.

56. Hempel, *Literatur* (1930), p. 94; Hertzberg, *Samuelbücher* (1960), pp. 232–234; *Samuel* (1964), pp. 281–283 maintains that the purpose of the story of David is to establish him as a man whose personality combines cultic, political and spiritual leadership. However, he bases this primarily on 2 Sam. 7 and not on 2 Sam 5. Grønbaek, *Aufstieg* (1971), p. 239 argues that 2 Sam. 5 is part of a unit based on an older story and adopted by the editor to his purpose, i.e., to show that all history is a fulfilment of God's will.

CONCLUSION

A careful study of the accounts and stories about David after he became king of all Israel shows the major message they contain to be a theological one. The lesson we are taught is that David brought about a radical change in the concept of the deity. Bringing the Ark up to Jerusalem, David's desire to build a permanent domicile for the Lord, and the acquisition of the Araunah threshing floor are all part of an effort to change the nature of the deity from an 'itinerant' God to a 'permanently settled' one. The first manifestation of the change is the end of the Lord's outbursts of rage. Consequently one may surmise that turning the 'wandering' God into a 'dwelling' one indicates that the Lord has stopped being capricious and demonic. Moreover, after the Ark is brought up to Jerusalem, there is no more evidence of David's asking the Lord for guidance, and thus, by the very nature of things, there is no further sign of direct, open Divine intervention in the course of the events described in 2 Samuel 5.

The changes in behaviour that accompany the change in the nature of the Deity are dealt with in detail in 2 Samuel 7, and the consequences are implied by the messages in 2 Samuel 5 and 8. From now on, not only does God refrain from destructive outbursts of rage, but His ways are predictable, His penalties 'human' and readily comprehensible (see, for example, 2 Samuel 7: 14–15 and also p. 99 above), and He is accessible and responsive to all.

Furthermore, besides direct responses, there are also responses transmitted through the 'man of God', who acts as mediator. The mediation is not accompanied by ominous signs and mysterious miracles.[1] All in all, it is reasonable to assume that the fact that the Deity very rarely intervenes in the course of events is another manifestation of a single, overall concept. This includes the special close relationship between God and David which is guaranteed to last forever and the Lord's constant, open and non-cryptic response to His people.[2]

The story of the change is told in 2 Samuel chapters 6, 7 and 24, while chapters 5 and 8 constitute, in the present form of the book, a literary framework for David's works. Chapters 6 and 24 contain the stories of the first and the last of his significant acts as king. It is hardly plausible that it was by accident that the editor-author used for his framework two events: one dealing with the cessation of the Lord's outbursts of rage, the other related to his ceasing to be a wandering God. The intention of this editing becomes even clearer against the background of the generally accepted hypothesis, that the order of events was in fact different from the order presented in the book of Samuel. From a historical point of view, the proper place for the story of Nathan's prophecy is after the purchase of the Araunah threshing floor and the establishment of the altar there.

The three chapters — 6, 7, and 24 — reflect the tension between traditional concepts and new ideas, as well as fear of the latter. Resistance and apprehension, it would seem, are the bases for the story of Uzzah, the story of the plague and the opposition to the building of the Temple.

1. It is instructive to note the difference between Samuel's behaviour towards David, both with regard to the description of his anointing and of the other encounters (e.g., 1 Sam. 19:18–24), although the description of the anointing of David is devoid of all the mysterious elements present in 1 Sam. 10:2–9).
2. One may find support for this view from what is reflected by the Midrash and other traditional commentaries that try to explain the absence of an Urim and Thumim oracle from the short account of David's victories in chapter 8.

It is quite likely that the tension and the apprehension caused the steps connected with the change to be described as a sin that aroused the Lord's anger. But I have attempted to prove that the central message of the stories is rejection of the apprehension. This is achieved by stressing the fact that David turns the Divine wrath into a blessing. He stops the Divine outbursts and succeeds in obtaining a favourable response from God, who promises the eternity of the royal dynasty.

In the context it seems quite reasonable to interpret this promise, as a promise of the everlastingness of David's accomplishments. Preventing the construction of the Temple because of the ideology of the 'wandering God' on the one hand, and on the other the compensation for this prohibition in the form of the divine promise of the eternity of the House of David, prove the strength of the opposition to David's revolutionary innovations. It is reasonable to conclude that this was really what caused David to refrain from building the Temple and it is quite possible that this opposition was also responsible for other events recorded in the book of Samuel.

However, it is not the purpose of the present study to try to reconstruct what actually happened, but rather to understand what the text before us intended to convey.

The structure of 2 Sam. 5 and 8 stresses the commitment between the Lord and David. The main stress in chapter 5 is on David's recognition that in all his accomplishments, no matter what the sphere of activity, God has been at his side. Chapter 8 brings out the fact that all the fruits of David's successes have been dedicated to God, but the context makes it look like an account of the way God has kept his promise to David and responded to his prayer. The reciprocity in the relations between the Lord and David expresses the concept of mutual responsibility — also expressed in chapter 7 — that has been realized in practice by David. According to this concept, David's belief in the Lord and his view of his own successes as the realization of a Divine plan, guarantee the permanence of belief in, and worship of, the Lord.

In my opinion, then, the editor-author ascribes to David not only the creation of an infra-structure for the new concept and for a different type of belief in God, but also integrates David's organizational activities in the sphere of both ritual and government with his ideology. The radical transition from perception of the Deity as an entity whose wrath may strike suddenly, without rhyme or reason, to the new perception of that deity — is the basis and the meaning of the stories of bringing up the Ark, of the census, and of the purchase of the Araunah threshing floor. The various aspects of the concept of God as 'Dwelling in a house' are described in the stories of Nathan's prophecy and David's prayer, and appear clearly in the short accounts in 2 Sam chapters 5 and 8. In other words, in the present context, it seems to me that the internal organization of the regime, especially 2 Sam. 5:16–18, as well as its international relations, its consolidation, and the dedication of the fruits of victory to God — all serve the same literary purpose.

From the argumentation of Nathan in his prophecy as to a 'wandering' Deity (especially in 2 Sam. 7:6–7) and from the various traditions associated with the Ark, one can postulate with virtual certainty that the concept of the wandering God, with all it implies, is a vestige of tribal tradition. In the concept of God as dwelling in a house we can see the basic needs of a belief appropriate for the kingdom of David. A comparison with the book of Kings, may indicate that this concept was not accepted in the Northern Kingdom.

A verification of the theory that what distinguishes the different concepts of God is the result of David's enterprises, can be found in the accounts as analysed in this study. Further support for this conclusion is to be found in the descriptions of Samuel's behaviour towrds Saul. This behaviour resembles the characteristic actions of the man of God in the Northern Kingdom but is absent from Samuel's actions towards David.

BIBLIOGRAPHICAL ABBREVIATIONS

Abramsky, "Monarchy" (1974)

ש. אברמסקי, "לתפיסת המלוכה בספר שמואל ולרקעה ההיסטורי", בית מקרא כרך כ חוברת ס (ירושלים תשל"ה/1974), עמ' 87–128 [בגרסה שונה במעט בספרו מלכות שאול ומלכות דוד – ראשית המלוכה בישראל והשפעתה לדורות].

S. Abramsky, "Monarchy in the Book of Samuel and its Historic Background", *Beth Mikra* vol. 20 no. 60 (Jerusalem 1974), pp. 87–128 [Hebrew with English summary on p. 164; for a slightly different version see *Kingdom,* pp. 337–365].

Abramsky, "Historiography" (1977)

ש. אברמסקי, "מעשה אמנות והִיסטוריוגראפיה בסיפור מלכות דוד", בית מקרא כרך כב חוברת עא (ירושלים תשל"ז/1977), עמ' 453–472.

S. Abramsky, "Art and Historiography in the Story of David's Kingdom", *Beth Mikra* vol. 22 no. 71 (Jerusalem 1977), 453–472 [Hebrew].

Abramsky, *Kingdom* (1977)

ש. אברמסקי, מלכות שאול ומלכות דוד: ראשית המלוכה בישראל והשפעתה לדורות (ירושלים 1977).

S. Abramsky, *The Kingdom of Saul and the Kingdom of David: The Beginning of Kingship in Israel and its Influence on Generations to Come* (Jerusalem 1977), [Hebrew].

Adar, *Narrative* (1959)

Z. Adar, *The Biblical Narrative,* translated from the Hebrew edition of 1957 by M. Louvish (Jerusalem 1959).

Ahuvia, *As it is Written* (1977)

א. אהוביה, ככל הכתוב: הארות על כתובים במקרא (תל אביב 1977).

A. Ahuvia, *As it is Written...* (Tel Aviv 1977), [Hebrew].

Aharoni, *Archaeology* (1982)

Y. Aharoni, *The Archaeology of the Land of Israel: From the Prehistoric Beginnings to the End of the First Temple Period,* edited by Miriam Aharoni; translated from the Hebrew edition of 1972/1978 by A.F. Rainey (Philadelphia 1982).

Albright, *Samuel* (1961)

W.F. Albright, *Samuel and the Beginnings of the Prophetic Movement,* Goldenson Lecture for 1961 (Cincinnati 1961).

Albright, *Gods of Canaan* (1968)

W.F. Albright, *Yahweh and the Gods of Canaan: A Historical Analysis of Two Contrasting Faiths,* Jordan Lectures 1965 (London 1968).

Alt, *Staatenbildung* (1930)

A. Alt, *Die Staatenbildung der Israeliten in Palästina,* Reformationsprogramm der Universität Leipzig (Leipzig 1930), [= partly reprinted in: *KS zur Geschichte des Volkes Israel,* vol. 2 (München 1953), pp. 1–66].

Alt, "Königtum" (1951)

A. Alt, "Das Königtum in den Reichen Israel und Juda", *VT* vol. 1 (1951), pp. 2–22 [= *KS zur Geschichte des Volkes Israel* vol. 2 (München 1953), pp. 116–134].

Alt, "Monarchy" (1968)
A. Alt, "The Monarchy in the Kingdoms of Israel and Judah", English translation of "Königtum" (1951) by R.A. Wilson, in: *Essays on the Old Testament History and Religion* (New York 1968), pp. 311–335.

Amit, "Prophecy" (1983)
יאירה אמית, "תפקיד הנבואה והנביאים במשנתו של ספר דברי הימים", בית מקרא כרך כח חוברת צג (תשמ"ג/1983), עמ' 113–133.
Yairah Amit, "The Role of Prophecy and Prophets in the Book of Chronicles", *Beth Mikra* vol. 28 no. 93 (1983), pp. 113–133 [Hebrew with English summary on pp. 206–207].

Auerbach, *Wüste* (1936/1938)
E. Auerbach, *Wüste und Gelobtes Land,* vol. 1 second edition (Berlin 1938); vol. 2 (Berlin 1936).

Balentine, *Hidden God* (1983)
S.E. Balentine, *The Hidden God: The Hiding of the Face of God in the Old Testament,* Oxford Theological Monographs (Oxford 1983).

Bar-Efrat, "Succession" (1983)
ש. בר־אפרת, "'סיפור ירושת כסא המלוכה של דוד'; בדיקה מחודשת של סברה מקובלת", ספר יצחק אריה זליגמן, מאמרים במקרא ובעולם העתיק, כרך א (ירושלים תשמ"ג/1983), עמ' 185–211.
S. Bar-Efrat, "The 'Succession History' Reconsidered", in: *Festschrift I.L. Seeligmann: Essays on the Bible and the Ancient World,* edited by A. Rofé & Y. Zakovitch, vol. 1 (Jerusalem 1983), pp. 185–211 [Hebrew].

Bartal, *Saul* (1982)

א. ברטל, מלכות שאול: המלך הראשון בישראל (תל אביב תשמ"ב/1982).

A. Bartal, *The Kingdom of Saul* (Tel Aviv 1982) [Hebrew with English summary].

Barthélemy, *Critique Textuelle* (1982)

D. Barthélemy, *Critique textuelle de l'Ancien Testament,* OBO vol. 50 part 1 (Fribourg/ Göttingen 1982).

Baqon, "David" (1965)

י. בקון, "סיפורי דוד בספרי שמואל ודברי הימים", בית מקרא כרך יא חוברת כה/כו (ירושלים תשכ"ו/1965), עמ' 59–80.

I. Baqon, "The David Narratives in Samuel and Chronicles", *Beth Mikra* vol. 11 nos. 25/26 (Jerusalem 1965), pp. 59–80 [Hebrew].

Bellinger, *Psalmody and Prophecy* (1984)

W.H. Bellinger, *Psalmody and Prophecy,* Journal for the Study of the Old Testament Supplement Series vol. 27 (Shefield 1984).

Bendor, *BET-AB* (1986)

ש. בנדור, בית האב בישראל למן ההתנחלות ועד סוף ימי המלוכה: מבנה החברה הקדומה בישראל (חיפה תשמ"ז/1986).

S. Bendor, *The BET-AB in Israel from the Settlement to the End of the Monarchy: The Social Structure of Ancient Israel* (Haifa 1986), [Hebrew, to be published in English in: Jerusalem Biblical Studies vol. 7].

Bentzen, "Ark" (1948)

A. Bentzen, "The Cultic Use of the Ark in Samuel," *JBL* vol. 67 (1948), pp. 37–56.

Bickerman, "Cyrus" (1964)
E. Bickerman, "The Edict of Cyrus", *JBL* vol. 65 (1946), pp. 262–268.

Blank, "Curse" (1950)
S.H. Blank, "The Curse, the Blasphemy, the Spell, the Oath", *HUCA* vol. 23 (1950/1951), pp. 73–96.

Bleek, *Einleitung* (1878)
F. Bleek, *Einleitung in das Alte Testament,* fourth edition adapted by J. Wellhausen (Berlin 1878).

Blenkinsopp, "Kiriath-Jearim" (1969)
J. Blenkinsopp, "Kiriath-Jearim and the Ark", *JBL* vol. 88 (1969), pp. 143–156.

Blenkinsopp, *Gibeon* (1972)
J. Blenkinsopp, *Gibeon and Israel: The Role of Gibeon and the Gibeonites in the Political and Religious History of Early Israel,* The Society for Old Testament Study Monograph Series vol. 2 (Cambridge 1972).

Brichto, *Curse* (1968)
H.C. Brichto, *The Problem of 'Curse' in the Hebrew Bible,* JBL Monograph Series vol. 8 (Philadelphia 1968).

Bright, *History* (1972)
J. Bright, *A History of Israel,* second edition (London/Philadelphia 1972).

Brin, "Formula" (1972)
ג. ברין, "לתולדות הנוסחה 'הוא יהיה לי לבן – ואני אהיה לו לאב'", בתוך: המקרא ותולדות ישראל,

מחקרים במקרא ובספרות ימי בית שני לזכרו של י. ליוור בעריכת ב. אופנהיימר (תל אביב תשל"ב/1972), עמ' 57–64.

G. Brin, "The History of the Formula 'He Shall Be to Me a Son and I will Be to Him a Father'", in: *Bible and Jewish History,* dedicated to the Memory of Jacob Liver, edited by B. Uffenheimer (Tel Aviv 1972), pp. 57–64 [Hebrew with English summary on p. XI]

Bronner, *Elijah* (1968)

Leah Bronner, *The Stories of Elijah and Elisha as Polemics Against Baal Worship,* Pretoria Oriental Series vol. 6 (Leiden 1968).

Bronner, *Personalities* (1974)

L. Bronner, *Biblical Personalities and Archaeology* (Jerusalem 1974).

Buber, *Königtum Gottes* (1932)

M. Buber, *Königtum Gottes* (Berlin 1932).

Buber, *Moses* (1946)

M. Buber, *Moses: The Revelation and the Covenant* (first published Oxford 1946 under the title *Moses*; reprinted New York 1958).

Buber, *Moses* (1948)

M. Buber, *Moses* (Zürich 1948; Heidelberg 1952) [= *Werke* vol. 2 (München 1964), pp. 9–230].

Buber, "Sprache" (1964)

M. Buber, "Die Sprache der Botschaft", in: *Werke*, vol. 2; Schriften zur Bibel (München 1964), pp. 1095–1109.

Buber, "Leitwortstil" (1964)

M. Buber, "Leitwortstil in der Erzählung des Pentateuch", in: *Werke* vol. 2: Schriften zur Bibel (München 1964), pp. 1131–1149.

Buber, "Leitwort-Style" (1964)

מ. בובר, "סגנון המלה המנחה", בתוך: דרכו של מקרא, עיונים בדפוסי סגנון בתנ"ך (ירושלים 1964), עמ' 284–309.

M. Buber, "The Leitwort-Style", in: *Ways of the Bible: Studies in Style Types in the Bible* (Jerusalem 1964), pp. 284–309 [Hebrew].

Buber, "Language" (1964)

מ. בובר, "לשונה של בשורה", בתוך: דרכו של מקרא, עיונים בדפוסי סגנון בתנ"ך (ירושלים תשכ"ד/1964) עמ' 272–283.

M. Buber, "The Language of Message", in: *Ways of the Bible: Studies in Style Types in the Bible* (Jerusalem 1964), pp. 272–283 [Hebrew].

Budde, *Samuel* (1894)

K. Budde, *The Books of Samuel*, English translation by B.W. Bacon, The Sacred Books of the Old Testament (Leipzig/Baltimore/London 1894).

Budde, *Samuelbücher* (1902)

K. Budde, *Die Bücher Samuel*, Kurzer Hand-Commentar zur Alten Testament vol. 8, second edition (Tübingen/Leipzig 1902).

Campbell, "Ark" (1979)

A.F. Campbell, "Yahweh and the Ark: A Case Study in Narrative", *JBL* vol. 98 (1979), pp. 31–43.

Carlson, *David* (1964)
R.A. Carlson, *David, the chosen King: A Traditio-Historical Approach to the Second Book of Samuel,* translated by E.J. Sharpe & S. Rudman (Stockholm/Göteborg/Uppsala 1964).

Cassuto, "Baal" (1938/1975)
U. Cassuto, "The Palace of Baal in Tablet II AB of Ras Shamra", translated from the Hebrew edition of 1938 by I. Abrahams, in: *Biblical and Oriental Studies,* vol. 2 (Jerusalem 1975), pp. 113–139.

Cassuto, "Sequence" (1947/1973)
U. Cassuto, "The Sequence and Arrangement of the Biblical Sections", Paper read before the World Congress of Jewish Studies, Jerusalem 1947, translated into English by I. Abrahams in: *Biblical and Oriental Studies,* vol. 1 (Jerusalem 1973), pp. 1–6.

Cassuto, "Blessing" (1954)
מ.ד. קאסוטו, "ברכה", אנציקלופדיה מקראית כרך ב (ירושלים תשי"ד/1954), עמ' 354–358.
U. Cassuto, "Blessing", *Encyclopaedia Biblica* vol. 2 (Jerusalem 1954), pp. 354–358 [Hebrew].

Clements, *David* (1967)
R. Clements, *Abraham and David: Genesis 15 and its Meaning for the Israelite Traditions,* Studies in Biblical Theology, second series no. 5 (London 1967).

Coats, *Saga* (1985)
G.W. Coats, *Saga, Legend, Tale, Novella, Fable: Narrative Forms in Old Testament Literature,* JSOTSupp. vol. 35 (Sheffield 1985).

Cross, *Canaanite Myth* (1974)

F.M. Cross, *Canaanite Myth and Hebrew Epic: Essays in the History of the Religion of Israel* (Cambridge Mass. 1973).

de Wette, *Beiträge* (1806)

W.M.L. de Wette, *Beiträge zur Einleitung in das Alte Testament* (Halle 1806; reprinted Darmstadt 1971).

Dinur, "Jerusalem" (1946)

ב.צ. דינור, "הסיפור על כיבושה של ירושלים בימי דוד ומשמעותו ההיסטורית", ציון כרך יא (ירושלים תש"ו/1946) עמ' 153–167 [= במקרא ובדורותיו: מחקרים ועיונים להבנת המקרא ותולדות ישראל בתקופתו, כתבים היסטוריים כרך שלישי (ירושלים תשל"ז/1977), עמ' 110–129].

B. Dinur, "The Story of the Conquest of Jerusalem by David and its Historical Significance", *Zion* vol. 11 (1946), pp. 153–167 [= *Historical Writings* vol. 3 (Jerusalem 1977), pp.110–129].

Driver, *Notes* (1913)

S.R. Driver, *Notes on the Hebrew Text and the Topography of the Books of Samuel* (Oxford 1913).

Dunston, The Dark Side (1983)

R.C. Dunston, The Dark Side of God: The Antagonistic God in the Mosaic Traditions, Dissertation Southern Baptist Theological Seminary 1983.

Ehrlich, *Mikra ki-Pheschuto* (1900)

א. ארליך [= שבתי בן יום טוב אבן בודד], מקרא כפשוטו (ברלין תר"ס/1900).

A.B. Ehrlich, *Mikra ki-Pheschuto* (Berlin 1900), [Hebrew].

Eichrodt, *Theologie* (1948)
W. Eichrodt, *Theologie des Alten Testaments,* third edition (Berlin 1948).

Eichrodt, *Theology* (1961)
W. Eichrodt, *Theology of the Old Testament,* English translation by J. Baker of the sixth German edition of *Theologie* (Stuttgart/Göttingen 1959), Old Testament Library (London 1961).

Eissfeldt, *Komposition* (1931)
O. Eissfeldt, *Die Komposition der Samuelbücher* (Leipzig 1931).

Eissfeldt, *Einleitung* (1956)
O. Eissfeldt, *Einleitung in das Alte Testament,* second edition (Tübingen 1956).

Eissfeldt, *Introduction* (1965)
O. Eissfeldt, *The Old Testament: An Introduction,* translated from the third German edition of 1964 by P.R. Ackroyd (Oxford 1965; reprinted New York 1976).

Eitrem, "Curses" (1970)
S. Eitrem, "Curses", *The Oxford Classical Dictionary* (Oxford 1970), pp. 302–303.

Euler, "Königtum" (1938)
K.F. Euler, "Königtum und Götterwelt in den altaramäischen Inschriften Nordsyriens. Eine Untersuchung zur Formsprache der

altaramäischen Inschriften und des Alten Testaments", *ZAW* vol. 56 (1938), pp. 272–313.

Fitzmyer, *Inscriptions* (1967)
J.A. Fitzmyer, *The Aramaic Inscriptions of Sefire,* Biblica et Orientalia vol. 19 (Rome 1967).

Flanagan, Traditions (1970)
J.W. Flanagan, A Study of the Biblical Traditions Pertaining to the Foundation of the Monarchy in Israel, Dissertation, submitted to the Graduate School of the University of Notre-Dame, Notre Dame Indiana 1970.

Fokkelman, *Narrative Art* (1981)
J.P. Fokkelman, *Narrative Art and Poetry in the Books of Samuel: A Full Interpretation Based on Stylistic and Structural Analyses,* vol. 1 (Assen 1981).

Frankfort, *Kingship* (1948)
H. Frankfort, *Kingship and the Gods: A Study of Ancient Near Eastern Religion as the Integration of Society and Religion* (Chicago 1948).

Fretheim, "Ark" (1968)
T.E. Frethheim, "The Ark in Deuteronomy", *CBQ* vol. 30 (1968), pp. 1–14.

Galling, *Erwählungstraditionen* (1928)
K. Galling, *Die Erwählungstraditionen Israels,* BZAW vol. 48 (Giessen 1928).

Galling, "Stifter" (1950)
K. Galling, "Königliche und nichtkönigliche Stifter beim Tempel von Jerusalem", in:

Beiträge zur biblischen Landes und Altertumskunde (Stuttgart 1950), pp. 134–153.

Garsiel, *David* (1975)
מ. גרסיאל, מלכות דוד: מחקרים בהיסטוריה ועיונים בהיסטוריוגרפיה (תל אביב תשל"ה/1975).
M. Garsiel, *The Kingdom of David: Studies in History and Inquiries in Historiography* (Tel Aviv 1975), [Hebrew].

Gelander, Relations (1984)
S. Gelander, The Relations between Literary devices and Ideological Message, Dissertation Tel Aviv University 1984 [Hebrew with English summary].

Gese, "Davidsbund" (1964)
H. Gese, "Der Davidsbund und die Zionserwählung", *ZThK* vol. 61 (1964), pp. 12–21.

Ginsburg, *Keret* (1946)
H.L. Ginsberg, *The Legend of King Keret: A Canaanite Epic of the Bronze Age*, BASORSupp. nos. 2–3 (1946).

Goulder, *Korah* (1982)
M.D. Goulder, *The Pslams of the Sons of Korah,* JSOTSupp. vol. 20 (Sheffield 1982).

Gray, *Kings* (1964)
J. Gray, *I & II Kings,* The Old Testament Library (London l964).

Greenberg, *Exodus* (1969)
M. Greenberg, *Understanding Exodus,* The Heritage of Biblical Israel, vol. 2 part 1 of the

Melton Research Center Series (New York 1969), pp. 110–113.

Greenberg, "Religion" (1979)
M. Greenberg, "Religion: Stability and Ferment", in: *The World History of the Jewish People,* First Series: Ancient Times, edited by B. Mazar, vol. 4,2 *The Age of the Monarchies: Culture and Society,* edited by A. Malamat, (Jerusalem 1979), pp. 79–123.

Greenberg, "Prayers" (1982)
מ. גרינברג, "תבניתה של תפילת הבקשה במקרא", ארץ ישראל כרך טז (ירושלים תשמ"ב/1982), עמ' 47–55.
M. Greenberg, "The Patterns of Prayers of Petition in the Bible", *Eretz Israel,* vol. 16 (1982), pp. 47–55 [Hebrew with English Summary on p. 253].

Gressmann, *Geschichtsschreibung* (1910)
H. Gressmann, *Die älteste Geschichtsschreibung und Prophetie Israels,* Die Schriften des Alten Testaments in Auswahl [= SAT], edited by H. Gressmann & H. Gunkel, vol. II,1 (Göttingen 1910).

Grintz, "David" (1969)
י.מ. גרינץ, "לתיאור חיי דוד בספר שמואל ובספר דברי הימים", בתוך: מוצאי דורות: מחקרים בקדמוניות המקרא וראשית תולדות ישראל וספרותו (תל אביב תשכ"ט/1969), עמ' 344–353.
Y.M. Grintz, "The Life of David acording [sic!] to the Book of Samuel and 1 Chronicles", in: *Studies in Early Biblical Ethnology and History* (Tel Aviv 1969), pp. 344–353 [Hebrew].

Grønbaek, *Aufstieg* (1971)
J.H. Grønbaek, *Die Geschichte vom Aufstieg Davids (1 Sam 15 — 2 Sam 5): Tradition und Komposition,* Acta Theologica Danica vol. 10 (Copenhagen 1971).

Gunkel, *Märchen* (1917)
H. Gunkel, *Das Märchen im Alten Testament* (Tübingen 1917).

Gunkel, *Genesis* (1964)
H. Gunkel, *Genesis,* Göttinger Handkommentar zum Alten Testament, vol. 1 sixth edition (Göttingen 1964).

Gunkel, *Legends* (1966)
H. Gunkel, *The Legends of Genesis: The Biblical Saga & History,* Translated from the German Edition of 1901 by W.H. Carruth (New York 1966), pp. 13–87.

Gunn, *Story* (1978)
D.M. Gunn, *The Story of King David: Genre and Interpretation,* JSOTSupp. vol. 6 (Sheffield 1978).

Gunneweg, *Leviten* (1965)
A.H.J. Gunneweg, *Leviten und Priester: Hauptlinien der Traditionsbildung und Geschichte des israelitisch-jüdischen Kultpersonals,* FRLANT vol. 89 (Göttingen 1965).

Haran, *Temples* (1978)
M. Haran, *Temples and Temple-Service in Ancient Israel: An Inquiry into the Character of Cult Phenomena and the Historical Setting of the Priestly School* (Oxford 1978).

Haran, "Composition" (1979)

מ. הרן, "סוגיות מקרא: מבעיות הקומפוזיציה של ספר מלכים ושל ספרי נביאים ראשונים", תרביץ כרך לז (תשכ"ח/1967), עמ' 1–14 [= מיקראה בחקר המקרא, בעריכת מ. ויינפלד, ליקוטי תרביץ כרך א (ירושלים תשל"ט/1979), עמ' 155–168].

M. Haran, "The Composition of the Book of Kings", *Tarbiz* vol. 37 (1967), pp. 1–14 [Hebrew; reprinted in: *A Biblical Studies Reader*, edited by M. Weinfeld, Likkutei Tarbiz (Jerusalem 1979), pp. 155–1168].

Hasel, "Nagid" (1984)

G.F. Hasel, "נגיד", *Theologisches Wörterbuch zum Alten Testament*, edited by J. Botterweck et al., vol. 5 Lieferung 1/2 (Stuttgart 1984), pp. 203–219.

Hempel, *Literatur* (1930)

J. Hempel, *Die Althebraeische Literatur und ihr helenistisch-jüdisches Nachleben*, Handbuch der Literaturwissenschaft (Wildpark-Potsdam 1930).

Hempel, *Geschichten* (1964)

J. Hempel, *Geschichten und Geschichte im Alten Testament* (Gütersloh 1964).

Herrmann, *Geschichte* (1973)

S. Herrmann, *Geschichte Israels in alttestamentlicher Zeit* (München 1973).

Herrmann, *History* (1975)

S. Herrmann, *A History of Israel in Old Testament Times*, translated from the German edition of 1973 by J. Bowden (Philadelphia 1975).

Hertzberg, *Samuelbücher* (1960)
H.W. Hertzberg, *Die Samuelbücher*, Das Alte Testament Deutsch vol. 10, second edition (Göttingen 1960).

Hertzberg, *Samuel* (1964)
H.W. Hertzberg, *1 & 2 Samuel*, translated by J.S. Bowden from the second German edition, The Old Testament Library (London 1964).

Herzog-Gichon, *Battles* (1978)
C. Herzog & M. Gichon, *Battles of the Bible* (Jerusalem 1978).

Hoffman, *Exodus* (1983)
י. הופמן, יציאת מצרים באמונת המקרא (תל אביב תשמ"ג/1983).
Y. Hoffman, *The Doctrine of the Exodus in the Bible* (Tel Aviv 1983), [Hebrew with English Summary on pp. 230–234].

Ishida, "Solomon's Succession" (1982)
T. Ishida, "Solomon's Succession to the Throne of David — A Political Analysis", in: *Studies in the period of David and Solomon and other Essays*, Papers Read at the International Symposium for Biblical Studies, Tokyo 5–7 December 1979, edited by T. Ishida (Winona Lake IN 1982), pp. 175–187.

Japhet, *Chronicles H* (1977)
שרה יפת, אמונות ודעות בספר דברי הימים ומקומן בעולם המחשבה המקראית (ירושלים תשל"ז/1977).
Sara Japhet, *The Ideology of the Book of Chronicles and Its Place in Biblical Thought* (Jerusalem 1977), [Hebrew].

Japhet, *Chronicles ET* (1989)
Sara Japhet, *The Ideology of the Book of Chronicles and Its Place in Biblical Thought,* translated from the Hebrew by Anna Barker, BEATJ vol. 9 (Frankfurt am Main/Bern/New York/Paris 1989).

Jeremias, "Lade" (1971)
J. Jeremias, "Lade und Zion: Zur Entstehung der Ziontradition", *Festschrift G. von Rad: Probleme biblischer Theologie,* edited by H.W. Wolff (München 1971), pp. 183–198.

Jeremias, *Königtum Gottes* (1987)
J. Jeremias, *Das Königtum Gottes in den Pslamen* FRLANT vol. 141 (Göttingen 1987).

Johnson, *Kingship* (1955)
A.R. Johnson, *Sacral Kingship in Ancient Israel* (Cardiff 1955).

Kallai, "Baal-perazim" (1954)
ז. קלאי־קליינמן, "בעל פרצים", אנציקלופדיה מקראית כרך ב (ירושלים תשי"ד/1954), עמ' 290–291.
Z. Kallai-Kleinmann, "Baal-perazim", *Encyclopaedia Biblica* vol. 2 (Jerusalem 1954), pp. 290–291 [Hebrew].

Kallai, *Historical Geography* (1986)
Z. Kallai, *Historical Geography of the Bible: The Tribal Territories of Israel* (Jerusalem/Leiden 1986).

Kaufmann, *Religion* (1947)
י. קויפמן, תולדות האמונה הישראלית מימי קדם עד סוף בית שני, מהדורה שניה כרך שני ספר ראשון [=ספר רביעי], (תל אביב תש"ז/1947).

Y. Kaufmann, *History of the Religion of Israel* (Tel Aviv 1947), [Hebrew].

Kaufmann, "David" (1957)

י. קויפמן, ״הספורים על דוד ושלמה״, מולד כרך טו (תל אביב תשי״ז/1967), עמ׳ 97–102 [= מכבשונה של היצירה המקראית (תל אביב תשכ״ו/1966), עמ׳ 168–179].

Y. Kaufmann, "The David and Solomon Stories", *Molad* vol. 15 (Tel Aviv 1957), pp. 97–102 [Hebrew; reprinted in: *From the Furnace of biblical Writing* (Tel Aviv 1966), pp. 169–179].

Kegler, *Politisches Geschehen* (1977)

J. Kegler, *Politisches Geschehen und Theologisches Verstehen* (Stuttgart 1977).

Kenyon, *Royal Cities* (1971)

K. Kenyon, *Royal Cities of the Old Testament* (London 1971).

Kittel, *Geschichte* (1923)

R. Kittel, *Geschichte des Volkes Israel,* fifth/sixth edition (Stuttgart 1923).

Kraus, *Königshaft* (1951)

H.J. Kraus, *Die Königshaft Gottes* (München 1951).

Labuschagne, *Incomparability* (1966)

C.J. Labuschagne, *The Incomparability of Yahweh in the Old Testament,* Pretoria Oriental Series vol. 5 (Leiden 1966).

Licht, "Miracle" (1968)

י. ליכט, ״נס, נסים״, אנציקלופדיה מקראית כרך ה (ירושלים תשכ״ח/1968), עמ׳ 874–879.

J. Licht, "Miracle, Miracles", *Encyclopaedia Biblica* vol. 5 (Jerusalem 1968), pp. 874–879 [Hebrew].

Licht, "Mimesis" (1976)

י. ליכט, "מימזיס כתכונה של הסיפור המקראי", בתוך: הצבי ישראל: אסופת מחקרים במקרא לזכר ישראל ברוידא ובנו צבי ברוידא, בעריכת י. ליכט וג. ברין (תל אביב תשל"ו/1976), עמ' 133–142.

J. Licht, "Mimesis in the Bible", in: *HATZVI ISRAEL: Studies in Bible [sic!] dedicated to the Memory of Israel and Zvi Broide,* edited by J. Licht & G. Brin (Tel Aviv 1976), pp. 133–142 [Hebrew].

Licht, *Storytelling* (1978)

J. Licht, *Storytelling in the Bible* (Jerusalem 1978).

Licht, "Establishment" (1980)

י. ליכט, "טענת הכינון המקראית", שנתון כרך ד (ירושלים תש"ם/1980), עמ' 98–128.

J. Licht, "The Biblical Claim of Establishment", *Shnaton,* vol.4 (Jerusalem 1980), pp. 98–128 [Hebrew with English summary on pp. VII–VIII].

Licht, *Numbers* (1985)

י. ליכט, פירוש על ספר במדבר [א–י] (ירושלים תשמ"ה/1985).

J. Licht, *A Commentary on the Book of Numbers [I–X],* (Jerusalem 1985) [Hebrew].

Liver, "Korah" (1961)

J. Liver, "Korah, Dathan and Abiram", *Scripta Hierosolymitana* vol. 8 (Jerusalem 1961), pp. 189–217.

Liver, "Kings" (1962)

י. ליוור, "מלכים", אנציקלופדיה מקראית כרך ד (ירושלים תשכ"ג/1962), עמ' 1129–1154.

J. Liver, "Kings", *Encyclopaedia Biblica* vol. 4 (Jerusalem 1962), pp. 1129–1154 [Hebrew].

Liver, "Anointing" (1968)

י. ליוור, "משיחה", אנציקלופדיה מקראית כרך ה (ירושלים תשכ"ח/1968) עמ' 526–531.

J. Liver, "Anointing", Encyclopaedia Biblica vol. 5 (Jerusalem 1968), pp. 526–531 [Hebrew].

Liver, "Nagid" (1968)

י. ליוור, "נגיד", אנציקלופדיה מקראית כרך ה (ירושלים תשכ"ח/1968), עמ' 753–755.

Y. Liver, "Nagid", *Encyclopaedia Biblica* vol. 5 (Jerusalem 1968), pp. 753–755 [Hebrew].

Loewenstamm, "Census" (1968)

ש.א. ליונשטאם, "מפקד", אנציקלופדיה מקראית כרך ה (ירושלים תשל"ח/1968), עמ' 218–221.

S.E. Loewenstamm, "Census", *Encyclopaedia Biblica* vol. 5 (Jerusalem 1968), pp. 218–221 [Hebrew].

Loewenstamm, "Tabernacle" (1968)

ש.א. ליונשטאם, "משכן ה'", אנציקלופדיה מקראית כרך ה (ירושלים תשכ"ח/1968), עמ' 532–548.

S.E. Loewenstamm, "Tabernacle", *Encyclopaedia Biblica* vol. 5 (Jerusalem 1968), pp. 532–548 [Hebrew].

Lohfink, "Individum" (1960)

N. Lohfink, "Wie stellt sich das problem Individum-Gemeinschaft im Deuteronomium", *Scholastik* vol. 35 (1960), pp. 403–407.

Lotz, "Bundeslade" (1901)

W. Lotz, "Die Bundeslade", *Festschrift Prinzregenten Luitpold von Bayern zum 80 Geburtstag,* Theologische Fakultät der Universität Erlangen (Leipzig 1901).

Luriah, *Benjamin* (1970)

ב.צ. לוריא, שאול ובנימין: מחקרים בתולדות שבט בנימין, כתבי החברה לחקר המקרא בישראל ספר כב (ירושלים תש"ל/1970).

B.Z. Luriah, *Saul and Benjamin: Studies in the History of the Tribe of Benjamin* (Jerusalem 1970) [Hebrew].

Maier, *Ladeheiligtum* (1965)

J. Maier, *Das altisraelitische Ladeheiligtum,* BZAW vol. 93 (Berlin/New York 1965).

Malamat, "Statecraft" (1970)

A. Malamat, "Organs of Statecraft in the Israelite Monarchy", *The Biblical Archaeologist Reader* vol. 3 edited by E.F. Campbell & D.N. Freedman (Garden City, NY 1970), pp. 163–198.

Malkiel, "Ark" (1962)

א. מלכיאל, "העלאת הארון מקרית יערים על ידי דוד", ספר מ. זיידל, פרסומי החברה לחקר המקרא בישראל כרך יא (ירושלים תשכ"ב/1962), עמ' 119–141.

A. Malkiel, "David's bringing up the Ark from Kiriath-Yearim", *Festschrift M. Seidel* (Jerusalem 1962), pp. 119–141, [Hebrew].

Mazar, "David's Reign" (1963)

B. Mazar, "David's Reign in Hebron and the Conquest of Jerusalem", *Festschrift A.H. Silver: In the Time of Harvest,* edited by S.B. Freehof (New York 1963), pp. 235–244.

Mazar, "Philistines" (1971)
B. Mazar, "The Philistines and their Wars with Israel", *The World History of the Jewish People,* first series vol. 3: *Judges,* edited by B. Mazar (Tel Aviv 1971), pp. 164–179.

Mazar, "Kingship" (1973)
ב. מזר, "המלוכה בישראל", בתוך: טיפוסי מנהיגות בתקופת המקרא, יום עיון לרגל מלאת שמונים וחמש שנים לדוד בן גוריון, ג דחנוכה תשל"ב (ירושלים תשל"ג/1973).
B. Mazar, "Kingship in Israel", in: *Types of Leadership in the Biblical Period,* Publications of the Israel Academy of Sciences and Humanities: A Study Conference in Honour of the Eighty-Fifth Birthday of David Ben-Gurion, held 15 December 1971 (Jerusalem 1973).

Mazar, "David and Solomon" (1979)
B. Mazar, "The Era of David and Solomon", *The World History of the Jewish People,* First Series Ancient Times edited by B. Mazar, vol. 4,1 *The Age of the Monarchies: Political History,* edited by A. Malamat (Jerusalem 1979), pp. 76–100.

McCarter, "Apology" (1980)
P.K. McCarter, "The Apology of David", *JBL* vol. 99 (1980), pp. 489–504.

McCarter, *II Samuel* (1984)
P.K. McCarter, *II Samuel,* The Anchor Bible vol. 9 (Garden City, New York 1984).

McCarthy, "Deuteronomistic History" (1965)
D.J. McCarthy, "2 Samuel and the Structure of Deuteronomistic History", *JBL* vol. 84 (1965), pp. 131–138.

McCarthy, "Wrath" (1974)
D.J. McCarthy, "The Wrath of Jahweh and the Structural Unity of the Deuteronomistic History", *Essyas in Old Testament Ethics,* edited by. J.L. Crenshaw & J.T.Willis (New York 1974), pp. 99–110.

McKenzie, "Dynastic Oracle" (1947)
J.L. Mckenzie, "The Dynastic Oracle, 2 Samuel 7", *Theological Studies* vol. 8 (1947), pp. 181–226.

McKenzie, "Elders" (1959)
J.L. McKenzie, "The Elders in the Old Testament", *Analecta Biblica* vol. 10 (Rome 1959), pp. 388–406.

Mendenhall, "Political Society" (1960)
G.E. Mendenhall, "The Relation of the Individual to Political Society in Ancient Israel", *Biblical Studies in Memory of H.C. Alleman,* edited by J.M. Myers et al., Gettysburg Theological Studies (New York 1960), pp. 89–108.

Mettinger, *King and Messiah* (1976)
T.N.D. Mettinger, *King and Messiah: The Civil and Sacral Legitimation of the Israelite Kings,* Coniectanea Biblica OT vol. 8 (Lund 1976).

Milgrom, *Terminology* (1970)
J. Milgrom, *Studies in Levitical Terminology, I: The Encroacher and the Levite. The Term 'Aboda,* University of California Publications, Near Eastern Studies vol. 14 (Berkley/Los Angeles/London 1970).

Montgomery, *Kings* (1951)
J.A. Montgomery, *A Critical and Exegetical Commentary on the Books of Kings,* edited by H.S. Gehman, ICC (Edinburgh 1951).

Morenz, "Königsliteratur" (1954)
S. Morenz, "Aegyptische und Davidische Königsliteratur", *Zeitschrift für aegyptische Sprache und Altertumskunde* vol. 79 (Berlin 1954), pp. 73–85.

Mosis, *Untersuchungen* (1973)
R. Mosis, *Untersuchungen zur Theologie des chronistischen Geschichtswerkes* (Freiburg im Breisgau 1973).

Na'aman, *Borders* (1986)
N. Na'aman, *Borders and Districts in Biblical Historiography,* Jerusalem Biblical Studies vol. 4 (Jerusalem 1986).

Newsome, "New Understanding" (1975)
J.D. Newsome, "Toward a New Understanding of the Chronicler and his Purpose", *JBL* vol. 94 (1975), pp. 201–217.

Nicholson, *Exodus* (1973)
E.W. Nicholson, *Exodus and Sinai in History and Tradition* (Oxford 1973).

North, "Kingship" (1932)
C.R. North, "The Religious Aspects of Hebrew Kingship", *ZAW* vol. 50 (1932), pp. 8–38.

Noth, *System* (1930)
M. Noth, *Das System der Zwölf Stämme Israels*, Beiträge zur Wissenschaft vom Alten und Neuen Testament [=BWANT] vol. 52 (Stuttgart 1930), [= in: *Geschichte Israels,* third edition (Göttingen 1956), pp. 83–194].

Noth, *Studien* (1943)
M. Noth, *Überlieferungsgeschichtliche Studien* (Halle an der Saale 1943; reprinted Tübingen 1957; Darmstadt 1963).

Noth, *Pentateuch* (1948)
M. Noth, *Überlieferungsgeschichte des Pentateuch*, (Stuttgart 1948).

Noth, "Jerusalem" (1950)
M. Noth, "Jerusalem und die israelitische Tradition", *OTS* vol. 8 (1950), pp. 28–46 [= Gesammelte Studien zum Alten Testament (München 1960), pp. 172–187].

Noth, *Geschichte* (1950)
M. Noth, *Geschichte Israels* (Göttingen 1950).

Noth, "Gott, König, Volk" (1950)
M. Noth, "Gott, König, Volk im Alten Testament: eine methodologische Auseinandersetzung mit einer gegenwärtigen Forschungsrichtung", *Zeitschrift für Theologie und Kirche* vol. 47 (Tübingen 1950), pp. 157–191 [= *Gesammelte Studien zum Alten Testament,* Theologische Bücherei vol. 6 (München 1957), pp. 188–229].

Noth, *History* (1958)
M. Noth, *The History of Israel,* translated from the second German edition of 1956 by S. Godman (New York 1958).

Noth, "God, King and Nation" (1966)
M. Noth, "God, King, and Nation in the Old Testament", in: *The Laws in the Pentateuch and other Studies,* Translated from the German by D.R. Ap-Thomas (Edinburgh/London 1966), pp. 145–178.

Noth, *Numeri* (1966)
M. Noth, *Das vierte Buch Mose: Numeri, übersetzt und erklärt,* Das Alte Testament Deutsch, vol. 7 (Göttingen 1966).

Noth, *Numbers* (1980)
M. Noth, *Numbers: A Commentary,* translated from the first German edition of 1966 by J.D. Martin, Old Testament Library, second edition (London/Philadelphia 1980).

Noth, *Pentateuchal Traditions* (1972)
M. Noth, *A History of Pentateuchal Traditions,* translated from the German edition of 1948, with an Introduction by B.W. Anderson (Englewood Cliffs NJ 1972).

Noth, *D History* (1981)
M. Noth, *The Deuteronomistic History,* translated by J. Doull et al. from the first part of the second German edition of *Studien* (1957), *JSOTSupp* no. 15 (Sheffield 1981).

Noth, *C History* (1981)
M. Noth, *The Chronicler's History,* translated by H.G.M. Williamson from the second part of the second German edition of *Studien* (1957), *JSOTSupp* vol. 50 (Sheffield 1987).

Nowack, *Samuelis* (1902)
W. Nowack, *Richter, Ruth und die Bücher Samuelis,* Handkommentar zum Alten Testament edited by D.W. Nowack, vol. 4 (Göttingen 1902).

Ota, "Note" (1974)
M. Ota, "A Note on 2 Samuel 7", *Festschrift J.M. Myers: A Light unto my Path,* edited by H.N. Bream et al. Gettysburg Theological Studies vol. 4 (Philadelphia 1974), pp. 403–407.

Otto, *Heilige* (1927)
R. Otto, *Das Heilige: über das Irrationale in der Idee des Göttlichen und sein Verhältniss zum Rationalen,* sixteenth edition (Gotha 1927).

Otto, *Holy* (1969)
R. Otto, *The Idea of the Holy*, English translation by J.W. Harvey (Oxford 1969).

Perry, "Literary Dynamics" (1979)
M. Perry, "Literary Dynamics: How the Order of Text Creates its Meanings", *Poetics Today* vol. 1 (Tel Aviv 1979), pp.35–64, 311–361.

Procksch, "David" (1913)
O. Procksch, "Die letzten Worte Davids", *Festschrift R. Kittel: Alttestamentliche Studien,* edited by A. Alt et al. BWAT vol. 13 (Leipzig 1913), pp. 113–125.

Razin, *Census* (1976)

מ. רזין, מפקדים ומגילות יחס ומשמעותם ההיסטורית לימי שאול ודוד, בעריכת ש. בנדור (חיפה תשל"ו/1976).

M. Razin, *Census Lists and Genealogies and their Historical Implications for the Times of David and Saul,* edited by S. Bendor (Haifa 1976), [Hebrew].

Reviv, *Clan* (1979)

ח. רביב, מבית אב לממלכה: ישראל בתקופת המקרא (ירושלים תשל"ט/1979).

H. Reviv, *From Clan to Monarchy: Israel in the Biblical Period* (Jerusalem 1979), [Hebrew].

Reviv, *Elders* (1989)

H. Reviv, *The Elders in Ancient Israel: A Study of a Biblical Institution,* translated from the Hebrew edition of 1983 by L. Plitmann (Jerusalem 1989).

Richter, "Nagid" (1965)

W. Richter, "Die Nagid Formel", *BZ* vol. 9 (1965), pp. 71–84.

Rofé, Angelology (1969)

א. רופא, האמונה במלאכים בישראל בתקופת בית ראשון לאור מסורות מקראיות, חיבור לשם קבלת תואר דוקטור, האוניברסיטה העברית בירושלים תשכ"ט/1969.

A. Rofé, Israelite Belief in Angels in the Pre-Exilic Period as Evidenced by Biblical Traditions, Dissertation The Hebrew University of Jerusalem 1969.

Rofé, "Rebekah" (1976)

א. רופא, "סיפור ארוסי רבקה (בראשית כד)", אשל באר שבע כרך א (באר שבע תשל"ו/1976), עמ' 42–67.

A. Rofé, "The Betrothal of Rebekah (Genesis 24)", *Eshel Beer-Sheva* vol. 1 (1976), pp. 42–67 [Hebrew].

Rofé, "David" (1986)

א. רופא, "מלחמת דוד בגלית – אגדה, תיאולוגיה ואסכטולוגיה", אשל באר שבע כרך ג (באר שבע תשמ"ו/ 1986), עמ' 55–90.

A. Rofé, "The Combat between David and Goliath – Legend, Theology and Eschatology", *Eshel Beer-Sheva* vol. 3 (1986), pp. 55–89.

Rofé, *Stories* (1988)

A. Rofé, *The Prophetical Stories: The Narratives about the Prophets in the Hebrew Bible, Their Literary Types and History,* translated from the Hebrew editions of 1982 & 1986 and revised (Jerusalem 1988).

Rohland, Erwähulungstradition (1956)

E. Rohland, Die Bedeutung der Erwählungstraditionen Israels für die Eschatologie der alttestamentlichen Propheten, Dissertation Heidelberg 1956.

Ross, "Yahweh Sebaoth" (1976)

J.P. Ross, "Yahweh Sebaoth in Samuel and Pslams", *VT* vol. 17 (1976), pp. 76–92.

Rost, *Thronnachfolge* (1926)

L. Rost, *Die Überlieferung von der Thronnachfolge Davids,* Beiträge zur Wissenschaft vom Alten und Neuen Testament [= BWANT], vol. III,6 (Stuttgart 1926); reprinted in: *Das Kleine Credo und andere Studien zum Alten Testament* (Heidelberg 1965), pp. 119–253.

Rost, *Succession* (1982)
L. Rost, *The Succession to the Throne of David,* English translation of *Thronnachfolge* by D. Rutter & D.M. Gunn (Sheffield 1982).

Rost, "Sinaibund" (1947)
L. Rost, "Sinaibund und Davidsbund", *TZ* vol. 72 (1947), pp. 129–134.

Rudolph, *Chronikbücher* (1955)
W. Rudolph, *Chronikbücher,* Handbuch zum Alten Testament, first series vol. 21 (Tübingen 1955).

Ruprecht, *Tempel* (1977)
K. Ruprecht, *Der Tempel von Jerusalem, Gründung Salomos oder jebusisches Erbe?* BZAW vol. 144 (Berlin/New York 1977).

Šanda, Könige (1911)
A. Šanda, *Die Bücher der Könige I,* Exegetisches Handbuch zum Alten Testament (Münster 1911).

Sarna, "Psalm 89" (1963)
N.M. Sarna, "Psalm 89: A Study in Inner Biblical Exegesis", in: *Biblical and Other Studies,* Studies and Texts vol. 1, edited by A. Altmann (Cambridge Mass. 1963), pp. 29–46.

Schmidt, "Kritik" (1971)
W.H. Schmidt, "Kritik am Königtum", *Festschrift G. von Rad*: *Probleme Biblischer Theologie,* edited by H.W. Wolff (München 1971), pp. 440–461.

Schmitt, *Zelt* (1972)
R. Schmitt, *Zelt und Lade als Thema alttestamentlicher Wissenschaft: Eine kritische forschungsgeschichtliche Darstellung* (Gütersloh 1972).

Schulte, *Geschichtschreibung* (1972)
Hannelis Schulte, *Die Entstehung der Geschcihtsschreibung im Alten Israel,* BZAW vol. 128 (Berlin/New York 1972).

Seeligmann, "Aetiology" (1961)
I.L. Seeligmann, "Aetiological Elements in Biblical Historiography", *Zion* vol. 26 (1961), pp. 141–169 [Hebrew with English summary on pp. I–II].

Seeligmann, "Erzählung" (1962)
I.L. Seeligmann, "Hebräische Erzählung und biblische Geschichtsschreibung", *Theologische Zeitschrift* vol. 18 (Basel 1962), pp. 305–325.

Seeligmann, "Cultic Tradition" (1964)
י.א. זליגמן, "מסורת פולחנית ויצירה היסטוריוגראפית במקרא", דת וחברה בתולדות ישראל ובתולדות העמים, קובץ הרצאות שהושמעו בכנס התשיעי לעיון בהיסטוריה (ירושלים תשכ"ה/1964), עמ' 41–61.
I.L. Seeligmann, "Cultic Tradition and historiographic Composition in the Bible", in: *Religion and Society,* Lectures delivered at the Ninth Convention of the Historical Society of Israel (Jerusalem 1964), pp. 41–61 [Hebrew].

Seeligmann, "Text" (1979)
י.א. זליגמן, "מחקרים בתולדות נוסחת המקרא", תרביץ כרך כה (תשט"ז/1956) עמ' 118–139; הודפס שנית עם השלמות בתוך: מיקראה בחקר המקרא, ליקוטי

תרביץ כרך א בעריכת מ. ויינפלד (ירושלים תשל"ט/1979), עמ' 255–278.

I.L. Seeligmann, "Studies in the History of the Biblical Text", *Likkutei Tarbiz* vol. 1: A Biblical Studies Reader Selected from Tarbiz — a quarterly for Jewish Studies, edited by M. Weinfeld (Jerusalem 1979), pp. 255–278 [Hebrew].

Segal, *Samuel* (1956)

מ.צ. סגל, ספרי שמואל ערוכים ומבוארים עם מבוא מפורט (ירושלים תשט"ז/1956).

M.Z. Segal, *The Books of Samuel — A Commentary* (Jerusalem 1965).

Sievers, *Samuel* (1907)

E. Sievers, *Metrische Studien III: Samuel,* Abhandlungen der Philologisch-historischen Klasse der Königlichen Sächsischen Gesellschaft der Wissenschaften, vol. 35 (Leipzig 1907).

Smend, *Jahwekrieg* (1966)

R. Smend, *Jahwekrieg und Stämmebund: Erwägungen zur ältesten Geschichte Israels*, Forschungen zur Religion und Literatur des Alten und Neuen Testaments vol. 84 (Göttingen 1966).

Smend, *Jahwe War* (1970)

R. Smend, *Jahwe War and Tribal Confederation: Reflections upon Israel's Earliest History,* translated from the second German edition of 1968 by M.G. Rogers (Nashville NJ 1970).

Smith, *Samuel* (1899)

H.P. Smith, *The Books of Samuel,* The International Critical Commentary (Edinburgh 1899).

Soederblom, *Gottesglauben* (1915)
N. Soederblom, *Das Werden des Gottesglauben: Untersuchungen über die Anfänge der Religion* (Leipzig 1915).

Soggin, *Königtum* (1967)
J.A. Soggin, *Das Königtum in Israel*, BZAW vol. 104 (Berlin/New York 1967).

Steuernagel, *Lehrbuch* (1912)
C. Steuernagel, *Lehrbuch der Einleitung in das Alte Testament* (Tübingen 1912).

Stoebe, "Jerusalem" (1957)
H.J. Stoebe, "Die Einnahme Jerusalems", *ZDPV* vol. 73 (1957), pp. 87–92.

Strikowsky, "Lord of Hosts" (1972)
א. סטריקובסקי, "תולדות השם צבאות בספר שמואל", בית מקרא כרך יז חוברת מט (ירושלים תשל"ב/1972), עמ' 183–192.
A. Strikowsky, "'The Lord of Hosts' in the Book of Samuel", *Beth Mikra* vol. 17 no. 49 (1972), pp. 183–192 [Hebrew with English summary on p. 258].

Tadmor, "Political Institutions" (1968)
H. Tadmor, "'The People' and the Kingship in Ancient Israel: The Role of Political Institutions in the Biblical Period", *Cahiers D'Histoire Mondiale,* vol. 11 nos. 1–2 (Neuchatel 1968), pp. 3–23.

Talmon, "Textual Study" (1975)
S. Talmon, "The Textual Study of the Bible — a New Outlook", in: *Qumran and the History of*

the Biblical Text, edited by F.M. Cross & S. Talmon (Cambridge Mass. 1975), pp. 321–400.

Thenius, *Bücher Samuels* (1842)
O. Thenius, *Die Bücher Samuels,* Kurzgefasstes exegetisches Handbuch zum Alten Testament, vierte Lieferung (Leipzig 1842).

Tiktin, *Untersuchungen* (1922)
H. Tiktin, *Untersuchungen zu den Büchern Samuelis,* Forschungen zur Religion und Literatur des Alten Testaments vol. 16 (Göttingen 1922).

Tsevat, "House of David" (1965)
M. Tsevat, "The House of David in Nathan's Prophecy", *Biblica* vol. 46 (1965), pp. 353–356.

Tur Sinai, *Peschuto* (1964)
נ.ה. טור סיני, פשוטו של מקרא: פירוש לסתומות שבכתבי הקודש לפי סדר הכתובים במסורת, כרך שני (ירושלים תשכ"ה/1964).
N.H. Tur Sinai, *Peschuto shel Miqra,* vol. 2 (Jerusalem 1964) [Hebrew].

Uffenheimer, "Policy" (1955)
ב. אופנהיימר, "יחס הנביאים לפוליטיקה החיצונית של אחאב", ספר א. אורבך, פרסומי החברה לחקר המקרא בישראל ספר א בעריכת א. בירם (ירושלים תשט"ו/1955), עמ' 84–93.
B. Uffenheimer, "The Prophets' Attitude to Ahab's Foreign Policy", *Festschrift E. Auerbach,* edited by A. Biram (Jerusalem 1955), pp. 84–93, [Hebrew].

Uffenheimer, "Prophecy" (1968)
ב. אופנהיימר, "נבואה, נביא", אנציקלופדיה מקראית כרך ה (ירושלים תשכ"ח/1968), עמ' 690–732.

B. Uffenheimer, "Prophecy", *Encyclopaedia Biblica* vol. 5 (Jerusalem 1968), pp. 690–732 [Hebrew].

Uffenheimer, *Ancient Prophecy* (1973)
ב. אופנהיימר, הנבואה הקדומה בישראל, (ירושלים תשל"ג/1973).
B. Uffenheimer, *Ancient Prophecy in Israel* (Jerusalem 1973) [Hebrew].

Uffenheimer, "Genesis 18–19" (1975)
B. Uffenheimer, "Genesis 18–19: A New Approach", *Festschrift Andre Neher* (Paris 1975), pp. 145–153.

Vanderkam, "Complicity" (1980)
J.C. Vanderkam, "Davidic Complicity in the Deaths of Abner and Eshbaal", *JBL* vol. 99 (1980), pp. 521–539.

Volz, *Das Dämonische* (1924)
P. Volz, *Das Dämonische in Jahwe*, Sammlung Gemeinverständlicher Vorträge und Schriften aus dem Gebiet der Theologie und Religionsgeschichte No. 110 (Tübingen 1924).

von Rad, "Königspsalmen" (1940)
G. von Rad, "Erwägungen zu den Königspsalmen", *ZAW* vol. 58 (1940/1941), pp. 216–222.

von Rad, "Königsritual" (1947)
G. von Rad, "Das judäische Königsritual", *Theologische Literaturzeitung* vol. 72 (1947), pp. 221–216 [= *Gesammelte Studien zum Alten Testament,* Theologische Bücherei vol. 8 (München 1958), pp. 205–213].

von Rad, *Hexateuch* (1938)
G. von Rad, *Das formgeschichtliche Problem des Hexateuch,* Beiträge zur Wissenschaft vom Alten und Neuen Testament vol. 4,26 (Stuttgart 1938), [= *Gesammelte Studien zum Alten Testament,* Theologische Bücherei vol. 8 (München 1958), pp. 9–86].

von Rad, "Hexateuch" (1966)
G. von Rad, "The Form-Critical Problem of the Hexateuch", in: *The Problem of the Hexateuch and Other Essays,* translated from the German by E.W. Trueman Dicken (London 1966; reprinted 1984), pp. 1–78.

von Rad, "Royal Ritual" (1966)
G. von Rad, "The Royal Ritual in Judah", in: *The Problem of the Hexateuch and Other Essays,* Translated from the German "Königsritual" (1947) by E.W. Trueman Dicken (London 1966; reprinted 1984), pp. 222–231.

von Rad, "Day of Yahweh" (1959)
G. von Rad, "The Origin of the Concept of the Day of Yahweh", *JSS* vol. 4 (1959), pp. 103–125.

von Rad, *Theologie* (1958/1960)
G. von Rad, *Theologie des Alten Testaments,* (München vol. 1 1958; vol. 2 1960).

von Rad, *Theology* (1962/1965)
G. von Rad, *Old Testament Theology,* translated from the German *Theologie* (1958/1960) by D.M.G. Stalker (Edinburgh/London vol. 1 1962; vol. 2 1965).

von Rad, "Zelt" (1931)
G. von Rad, "Zelt und Lade", *Neue Kirchliche Zeitschrift* vol. 42 (Leipzig 1931), pp. 476–498 [= in: *Gesammelte Studien zum Alten Testament,* Theologische Bücherei vol. 8 (München 1958), pp. 109–129].

von Rad, "Tent" (1966)
G. von Rad, "The Tent and the Ark", translated from the German "Zelt" (1931) by E.W. Trueman Dicken, in: *The Problem of the Hexateuch and Other Essays* (London 1966), pp. 103–124.

Ward, David's Rise (1967)
R.L. Ward, The Story of David's Rise: A Traditional-Historical Study of 1 Samuel XVI — 2 Samuel V, Dissertation Nashville Tennessee 1967.

Weinfeld, "Covenant" (1970)
M. Weinfeld, "The Covenant of Grant in the Old Testament and in the Ancient Near East", *JAOS* vol. 90 (1970), pp. 184–203.

Weinfeld, *Deuteronomy* (1972)
Deuteronomy and the Deuteronomic School (Oxford 1972).

Weinfeld, "Curse" (1976)
מ. ויינפלד, "קללה", אנציקלופדיה מקראית כרך ז (ירושלים תשל"ו/1976), עמ' 185–192.
M. Weinfeld, "Curse", *Encyclopaedia Biblica* vol. 7 (Jerusalem 1976), pp. 185–192 [Hebrew].

Weinfeld, *Justice* (1985)
מ. ויינפלד, משפט וצדקה בישראל ובעמים (ירושלים תשמ"ה/1985).

M. Weinfeld, *Justice and Righteousness in Israel and the Nations* (Jerusalem 1985), [Hebrew].

Weiser, *Glaube* (1931)

A. Weiser, *Glaube und Geschichte im Alten Testament,* BWANT vol. 4,4 (Stuttgart 1931); reprinted in *Glaube und Geschichte im Alten Testament und andere ausgewählte Schriften* (Göttingen 1961), pp. 99–182.

Weiser, "Tempelbaukrise" (1965)

A. Weiser, "Die Tempelbaukrise unter David", *ZAW* vol. 77 (1965), pp. 153–168.

Weisman, Charisma (1972)

ז. ויסמן, האישיות החריסמטית במקרא, חיבור לשם קבלת תואר דוקטור, האוניברסיטה העברית בירושלים 1972.

Z. Weisman, The Charismatic Personality in the Bible, Dissertation Hebrew University Jerusalem, 1972 [Hebrew].

Weisman, *Jacob* (1986)

ז. ויסמן, מיעקב לישראל: מחזור הסיפורים על יעקב שילובו בתולדות אבות האומה, (ירושלים תשמ"ו/1986).

Z. Weisman, *From Jacob to Israel: The Cycle of Jacob's Stories and its Incorporation within the History of the Patriarchs* (Jerusalem 1986) [Hebrew with detailed English Contents].

Weiss, "Law and Custom" (1976)

ר. וייס, "חוק ומנהג בספר שמואל", בתוך: משוט במקרא (ירושלים, ללא תאריך, כנראה תשל"ו), עמ' 10–15.

R. Weiss, "Law and Custom in the Book of Samuel", in: *MISHUT BAMIQRA: Biblical Studies* (Jerusalem, no date, probably 1976).

Wellhausen, *Samuel* (1871)
J. Wellhausen, *Der Text der Bücher Samuelis* (Göttingen 1871).

Wellhausen, *Composition* (1889)
J. Wellhausen, *Die Composition des Hexateuch und der historischen Bücher des Alten Testaments* (Tübingen/Leipzig 1889).

Whybray, *Succession* (1968)
R.N. Whybray, *The Succession Narrative: A Study of 2 Sam 9–20 and 1 Kings 1 & 2,* Studies in Biblical Theology, second series no. 9 (London 1968).

Wilcoxen, "Narrative" (1974)
J.A. Wilcoxen, "Narrative", in: *Old Testament Form Criticism* edited by J.H. Hayes (San-Antonio 1974), pp. 57–98.

Willi, *Auslegung* (1972)
Th. Willi, *Die Chronik als Auslegung: Untersuchungen zur literarischen Gestaltung der historischen Überlieferung Israels,* FRLANT vol. 106 (Göttingen 1972).

Yadin, "Blind & Lame" (1952)
י. סוקניק־ידין, "העורים והפסחים וכיבוש ירושלים", הכינוס העולמי הראשון למדעי היהדות, קיץ תש"ז (ירושלים תשי"ב/1952), עמ' 222–225.
Y. Sukenik-Yadin, "The Blind and Lame and the Conquest of Jerusalem", *Proceedings of the first World Congress of Jewish Studies held at the Hebrew University of Jerusalem, Summer 1947* (Jerusalem 1952), pp. 222–225 [Hebrew].

Zakovitch, "Story" (1983)
Y. Zakovitch, "Story versus History", *The Proceedings of the Eighth World Congress of Jewish Studies,* Panel Sessions (Jerusalem 1983), pp. 47–60.

Zimmerli, "Theologie" (1971)
W. Zimmerli, "Alttestamentliche Traditionsgeschichte und Theologie", *Festschrift G. von Rad: Probleme biblischer Theologie,* edited by H.W. Wolff (München 1971), pp. 637–647).

OTHER ABBREVIATIONS

ANET	*Ancient Near Eastern Texts Relating to the Old Testament,* edited by J.B. Pritchard (Princeton 1955).
ATD	*Das Alte Testament Deutsch,* Göttingen.
BASOR	Bulletin of the American Schools of Oriental Research, New Haven.
BASORSupp.	Bulletin of the American Schools of Oriental Research Supplementary Studies, (Jerusalem), New Haven.
BEATJ	Beiträge zur Erforschung des Alten Testaments und des Antiken Judentums, edited by M. Augustin, Frankfurt am Main / Bern / New York.
Beth Mikra	Beth Mikra Quarterly, Jerusalem [Hebrew].
Bib.	Biblica, Rome
BWANT	Beiträge zur Wissenschaft vom Alten und Neuen Testament, (Leipzig) Stuttgart.
BZ	Biblische Zeitschrift, (Freiburg im Breisgau) Paderborn.
BZAW	Beihefte zur Zeitschrift für die alttestamentliche Wissenschaft, (Giessen) Berlin/New York.
CBQ	The Catholic Biblical Quarterly, Washington D.C.

Eretz Israel (EI)	Eretz Israel, archaeological, historical and geographical studies, Jerusalem [Hebrew & English].
FRLANT	Forschungen zur Religion und Literatur des Alten und Neuen Testamentes, Göttingen.
HUCA	Hebrew Union College Annual, Cincinnati.
JAOS	Journal of the American Oriental Society, Boston.
JB	*The Jerusalem Bible,* edited by A. Jones, Garden City New York 1966.
JBL	Journal of Biblical Literature, USA.
JBS	Jerusalem Biblical Studies, Jerusalem.
JPS	The Holy Scriptures, the Jewish Publication Society of America, Philadelphia 1978.
JSOT	Journal for the Study of the Old Testament, Sheffield.
JSOTSupp.	Journal for the Study of the Old Testament Supplement Series.
JSS	Journal of Semitic Studies, Manchester.
KS	Kleine Schriften.
LXX	A. Rahlfs, *Septuaginta,* fifth edition (Stuttgart 1952).
MSS	Manuscripts.
MT	Masoretic Text.

NEB	The New English Bible, (Oxford/Cambridge 1970).
OTS	Oudtestamentische Studiën, Leiden.
RSV	The Revised Standard Version of the Bible.
Scripta	Scripta Hierosolymitana, publications of the Hebrew University, Jerusalem.
Shnaton	Shnaton, an Annual for Biblical and Ancient Near Eastern Studies, Jerusalem [Hebrew].
Tarbiz	Tarbiz, a Quarterly for Jewish Studies, Jerusalem [Hebrew].
VT	Vetus Testamentum, Leiden.
ZAW	Zeitschrift für die alttestamentliche Wissenschaft, (Giessen) Berlin/New York.
ZDPV	Zeitschrift des Deutschen-Palästina-Vereins, (Leipzig, Stuttgart), Wiesbaden.
Zion	Zion, a Quarterly for Research of Jewish History, Jerusalem [Hebrew].
ZThK	Zeitschrift für Theologie und Kirche, (Freiburg im Breisgau, Leipzig) Tübingen.

INDEX OF BIBLICAL PASSAGES

Genesis

6:1 25
12:13 115
12:15 115
15 76 82 103
16:4 46
20:11 43
24 73
26:9 43
32:2–3 131
33:16–17 131
39:9 43
49:16 89

Exodus

4:21 56
6:12 43
6:30 43
9:12 56
15:11 26
30 56
30:12 56
38:25–26 56

Leviticus

21:18 122

Numbers

1:2 56
11:28 34
12:7 23
16 65
16:22 65
24:3 121
24:15 121

Deuteronomy

2:25 96
3:20 82
3:24 26
12:10 82
19:6 116
24:1–3 30
25:18 43
25:19 82
28:65 96
29:9 89
32:25 34

Joshua

1:13 82
1:15 82
8:10 57
14:6 16
21:44 82
21:43 47
23:2 89
24:1 89

Judges

6:7–10 99
7:3 57
8:5–7 124
8:23 30
9:23 56
11:29–33 123
11:29 123
11:30–31 123
11:32 123
11:33 123
13:6 16
13:8 16

1 Samuel

1–3 80
1:7 80
2:25 56
2:35 23
4–6 35 36
6:12–15 35
6:19 35
7:3 47
9:2 34
9:8–9 16
9:20 17
10:2–10 18
10:2–9 138
10:2–6 17
13 27 131
13:11–12 27
13:15 57

15:4 56
15:11 25
15:24 13
19:18–24 138
20:15 51
21 117
22:1–5 129
23:17 51
24:11 52
24:20 51
25:28 23
25:30 51
26:9 52
26:11 52
28 17
28:6 12
28:19 12 17
28:20–23 17
29:6 116

2 Samuel
1–8 10 28 136
1–5 53 135
1 12 29 116
1:10 116
1:12 29 47
1:14 52
1:15 29
1:16 29 52
2:1 11 12
2:22 43
3 117 118
3:2–5 114 127
3:9–10 51 116
3:13–16 51 127
3:18 129
3:22 122
3:25 116
3:37 51–52
3:38 96 102
4 30 111 113
5–6 33
5 10 28 30 71 76 111–136 137 138 139 140
5:1–12 113
5:1–3 112 115 116 129
5:1–2 112 114 118
5:1 117
5:2 51 117 132 134
5:3 112 114 117
5:4–7 133
5:4–5 112 118 126
5:4 113 134
5:5 113
5:6–16 112
5:6–9 126
5:6–8 120 123
5:6 114 124 125
5:7 124
5:8 122 124 125
5:9–11 124
5:9 120 124
5:10 119 126 127 132 134
5:11–8:18 33
5:11–16 126
5:11–12 126
5:11 113
5:12 126 127 132 134
5:13–16 113 118 127 128
5:16–18 140
5:17–25 112 113 126 128 129 130
5:17–21 131
5:17 112 129
5:19–20 12
5:19 12 114–115 132
5:20 129 133 135
5:21 135
5:22–25 131
5:23–24 12 115 133
5:24 26–27 131 135
5:25 129 133
6–7 39
6 10 27 33–53 69–74 130 138
6:1–4 53
6:1 34
6:2–4 48
6:2 40 47
6:3 47
6:4 47
6:5 44 47 53
6:6–7 26
6:6 33 50
6:7 47 53
6:8 43 47 124

6:9–12 53
6:9 43
6:10–12 42 48
6:10 43 47
6:11–13 39
6:11 47
6:12 47
6:13–15 53
6:14–15 41 48
6:15 47
6:16 34 50
6:17–18 49
6:17 47
6:18 47
6:19 47
6:20–21 46 49
6:20 40 47 50 108
6:21 35 46 47 70
6:22 40 50
6:23 34 46 70
7–23 27
7 10 14 22 26 28 65 74 75–109 136 137 138 139
7:1–16 87
7:1–10 93
7:1–7 85 95
7:1 28 82 87 88 93
7:2 81 88 125
7:3 85
7:4 84 108
7:5–7 85
7:5–6 72
7:5 78 81 83 84 85 88
7:6–7 93 140
7:6 11 82 84 88 92
7:7 82 88 89 92 104
7:8–17 85
7:8–16 87
7:8–11 81 85
7:8–10 93
7:8 21 22 80 83 86 88 93
7:9–16 97
7:9 88 93 96 102
7:10–11 85 86 87
7:10 88 95 96
7:11–13 84
7:11–12 84 85
7:11 77 81 84 85 87 88 95 97 104
7:12–16 96 97
7:12–13 85
7:12 80 81 85 86 88 97 100
7:13 76 77 79 80 81 82 83 85 86 87 88 96 97 101 104
7:14–15 96 97 137
7:14 26 81 82 84 85 88 98 99
7:15 74 86 88 97 104
7:16–17 85
7:16 22 82 83 84 85 88 97 100–101
7:17 108
7:18–29 87
7:18–21 85
7:18 84 88 108
7:19 83 85 87 88
7:20 83 85
7:21 102
7:22–24 85 86
7:22 101 102
7:23–29 85
7:23–24 92
7:23 84 88
7:24–25 85
7:24 88
7:25–29 81–82
7:25 88 101
7:26 86 88 102–103
7:27 84 88
7:29 86 88 102
8 113 137 138 139 140
9–20 13 27
10:9 34
12 12
12:13 12 13
12:18 43
15:31 13
16:3 47
17:4 72
17:14 13
21 55 66 67
21:1 66 70

21:8 70
21:15–22 129 130
23:5 94 101
23:12–17 129
23:13 129
24 10 26 27 29 35 46 55–67 69–74 138
24:1 26 55 61
24:3 58
24:4 57 58 59
24:5–7 57 58
24:7 58
24:9 57 58 62
24:10 62
24:11 16
24:16 59–60
24:17 60 65 66
24:18–19 60
24:18 65–66
24:21 60 65–66
24:25 60 62

1 Kings
1–2 27
1:47 102
2:3–4 101
3:5 61
5:17 78
5:18 82
8 37
8:1 46
8:3 46
8:13 72
8:15 21
8:19 79
8:25 21 101
8:34 21
8:36 21
8:41 103
8:53 21
8:56 21
8:61 21
9:2 61
9:5–6 101
9:5 21
11:4 21
11:29–39 17 19 24
11:31–34 19
11:34 21
11:36 22
11:38 19 22
12:1–20 24
12:21 47
12:26–31 24
13 17
13:1–6 16
13:3–5 18
13:4 18
13:8–9 17
14 22
14:1–18 24
14:1–8 16
14:3 20
14:6 18 20
14:7 20 21 88–89
14:8–16 24
14:8 20 22
14:11 20
14:12 18
14:29 20
15:3–4 21
15:4 22
16:2 21 22 89
17:13 16
17:17–24 16
18:37–38 62
20 16
20:10–11 124
20:13–14 18
20:13 16
20:28 16 18
20:35–37 18
20:35 16
22:15 18
22:17 18

2 Kings
1 16 24
1:9–17 25
1:9–11 18
2 25
2:19–22 16
2:23–24 25
3:6 57
3:14–20 18
3:19–22 16
4 25
4:38–41 16
5 17 25
5:10 18
5:14 18
5:27 18
6:9–10 19
6:17 19
6:18 19
6:20 19
6:22 18

8:7–15 17
8:10 18
8:19 22 23
9:2–3 18
9:6 18
13:14–19 19
13:17 95
13:18–19 18
13:20–21 17
14:25–26 19
14:25 95
17:7–23 23
17:18 23
17:19 23
17:21 23
17:24–41 15
19:27 116
20:1–11 17

Isaiah
9:5 102
23:4 34
28:21 133
31:8 34
37:28 116
40:30 34
44:7 26
55:14 101

Jeremiah
3:16 37 45
10:7 103
23:21 101
48:15 34
49:19 26
49:26 34
50:30 34
51:22 34

Ezekiel
23:23 34

Amos
4:10 34
7:1–6 25

Micah
3:11–12 66
7:18 26

Psalms
2:8 98
6:5 103
23:3 103
25:7 103
25:11 103
31:4 103
35:10 26
42 41
44:27 103
46 37 41
47 41
48 37
48:12 103
69:25 25
69:28 25
71:19 26
76 37
78:31 34
79:9 103
84 41
87–89 41
89 94 102
89:4 101
89:9 26
89:25–37 94
89:29 101
89:40 94
106:8 103
113:5 26
121:8 116
132 37 45 94 102
143:11 103

Proverbs
20:29 34

Ecclesiates
11:9 34

Lamentations
1:15 34

Daniel
9:16 25

1 Chronicles
3:1–9 127
11–13 33
11:4–6 122 124
11:4 120
11:10–12:41 33 70
11:15–16 129
13–14 71
13:8 44
13:12 43
14:12 135
14:15 131

15:26 45
15:29 34
17:4 78
17:6 89
17:11 80
17:12 79 80
17:13 98 104
21 59 63
21:1 61
21:3 58
21:6 59
21:7 63
21:8 63
21:9 16
21:17 65
21:18 60
21:26 62
21:29–30 61
22:1 61
22:2–19 61
22:8 78
22:9–10 98
28:6 98

2 Chronicles
6:32 103
6:42 101
17:7–9 31
19:1–11 31
29–31 31
36:17 34

INDEX OF AUTHORS

Abrabanel, I. 13 36 56 77 78 79 90
Abramski, S. 12 51 77 83 86 104 114 116 126
Adar, Z. 13
Aharoni, Y. 125
Albright, W.F. 72 83
Alt, A. 10 25 31 58 73 83 88 101 117 119
Amit, Yaira 16
Auerbach, E. 13 35 66 122

Balentine, S.E. 73
Baqon, I. 44
Bar Efrat, S. 27
Bartal, A. 66
Barthélemy, D. 89
Bellinger, W.H. 94
Bendor, S. 58
Bentzen, A. 38
Bickerman, E. 90
Blank, S.H. 46
Bleek, F. 35 55 76 84
Blenkinsopp, J. 35 66
Brichto, H.C. 46
Bright, J. 56 66
Brin, G. 82 88 100
Bronner, Lea 17
Broshi, M. 57
Buber, M. 30 41 76 108
Budde, K. 12 28 33 35 55 85 112 116

Campbell, A. 36 52
Carlson, R.A. 12 35 38 39 83 84 95 96 121 126 130
Cassuto, U. 40 46 111
Clements, R. 37 38 76 82 103 118
Coats, G.W. 20
Cross, F.M. 56 94

David Kimhi – see: Radak
de Wette, L. 14
Dinur B.Z. 121 127
Driver, S.R. 66 78
Dunston, R.C. 26 44 72

Ehrlich, A. 29 44
Eichrodt, W. 23 25 26 30 31 37 38 39 44 46 56 66 71 73 74 97 99 100
Eissfledt, O. 38 86 116 119
Eitrem, S. 46
Euler, K.F. 100

Fitzmeier, J.A. 121
Flanagan, J.W. 53 71 77 86 87 119
Fokkelman, J.P. 12
Frankfort, H. 72
Fretheim, T.E. 38 45

Galbraith, J.A. 41
Galling, K. 55 94
Garsiel, M. 13 28 119
Gelander, S. 28
Gese, H. 83 100
Gichon, M. 122
Ginsberg, H.L. 39
Goulder M.D. 41
Gray, J. 18 21
Greenberg, M. 15 19 31 71 72 95 103
Gressmann, H. 35 85
Grintz, Y.M. 45
Grønbaek, J.H. 12 28 30 53 71 112 119 126 129 136
Gunkel, H. 20
Gunn, D.M. 10
Gunneweg, A.H.J. 36

Haran, M. 15 24 64
Hasel, G.F. 21
Hempel, J. 34 59 70 136
Hermann, S. 58
Hertzberg, H.W. 12 28 30 33 55 76 112 113 114 117 127 129 136
Herzog C. 122
Hoffman, Y. 15 84

Ishida, T. 73

Japhet, Sara 33 59 61 62 63 64 70 98
Jeremias, J. 37 38 41 45 83 100
Johnson, H.R. 55
Joseph Kara 36 78 120

Kallai, Z. 58 132
Kara – see: Joseph Kara
Kaufmann, Y. 27 36 44 72 86 90 91 96
Kegler, J. 38
Kenyon, K. 121 122
Kimhi – see: Radak
Kittel, R. 35 84
Kraus, H.J. 100

Labuschange, C.J. 26
Levi ben Gershom – see: Ralbag
Licht J. 27 56 57 92 123 124
Liver, J. 15 21 65 83 113
Loewenstamm, S.E. 57 82
Lohfink, N. 99
Lotz, W. 35
Luriah, B. 67 70

Maier, J. 45
Malamat, A. 46 72
Malkiel, A. 36
Mazar, B. 13 72 119 122
McCarter, P.K. 12 33 35 42 52 56 58 67 79 80 83 85 89 91 96 98 99 100 102 108 126

McCarthy, D.J. 28 39 76 77 82 99 103
McKenzie, J.L. 72 77 86 87
Mendenhall, G.E. 58
Mettinger, T.N.D. 87 114
Milgrom, J. 36 38 83
Montgomery, J.A. 21
Morenz, S. 99
Moses ben Nahman – see: Ramban
Mosis, R. 62

Na'aman, N. 58 69
Nahmanides – see: Ramban
Newsome, J.D. 62
Nicholson, E.W. 94
North, C.R. 29 39 82
Noth, M. 15 20 22 24 25 31 36 37 38 45 65 73 84 85 95 100 112 113
Nowack, W. 81

Ota, Michico 90
Otto, R. 15 26 72

Perry, M. 117
Procksch, O. 84 87

Radak [Rabbi David Kimhi] 30 36 56 62 111 135
Ralbag [Rabbi Levi ben Gershom] 30 55 56 75
Ramban [Rabbi Moshe ben Nahman] 56
Rashi [Rabbi Shlomo ben Itzhak] 30 44
Razin, M. 122 128 56 75 111
Reviv, H. 20 28 33 59 72 122 130
Richter, W. 83 100
Rofé, A. 15 16 17 18 19 20 24 56 60 61 63 73
Rohland, E. 37
Ross, J.P. 102 132
Rost, L. 10 13 27 34 52 74 77 81 85 86 87 93 96 97 104
Rudolph, W. 63
Ruprecht, K. 85

Šanda, A. 101
Sarna, N.K. 94
Schmidt, W.H. 66 76 94
Schmitt, R. 38
Schulte, Hannelis 50 116 126
Seeligmann, I.L. 40 80 131
Segal, M.L. 78 90
Shiloh, Y. 57
Sievers, E. 77 84 85 97
Smend, R. 37
Smith, H.P. 67 98 104 116
Soederblom, N. 15
Soggin, A. 12 83

Solomon ben Isaac – see: Rashi
Steuernagel, C. 35
Stoebe, H.J. 121
Strikowski, A. 102 132

Tadmor, H. 72
Talmon, S. 79 80
Thenius, O. 55 81
Tiktin, H. 81 85 97
Tsevat, M. 82
Tur Sinai, N.H. 35 122 124

Uffenheimer, B. 15 17 18 19 20 47 76 86

Vanderkam, J.C. 52 67
Volz, P. 44 45
von Rad, G. 15 21 24 31 34 37 38 40 55 57 58 64 73 80 85 87 94 97 99 102

Ward, R.L. 28 30 33 113 116 121 122 129
Weinfeld, M. 20 41 46 84 98 101
Weiser, A. 51 85 93
Weisman, Z. 83 91
Weiss, R. 130
Wellhausen, J. 66 76 87 112
Whybray, R.N. 13 23
Wilcoxen, J.A. 131
Willi, T. 63

Yadin, Y. 121
Yosef Kara – see: Joseph Kara

Zakovitch, Y. 23
Zimmerli, W. 10

HEBREW SECTION

ומאופן עריכתו, כגון שמ"ב ח. יחד עם המסופר בפרקים ו, ז, ו־כד, משתמע שהיחסים בין דוד לאלהיו יצרו מעין ערבות הדדית. אמונתו של דוד ובטחונו בה' מבטיחים את יציבותה ואת נצחיותה של ממלכתו, וארגונה ויציבותה של ממלכת דוד מבטיחים את נצחיות האמונה בה'.

לאידיאולוגיה של מפעל דוד השלכות מרחיקות לכת. היא היוותה את הבסיס לאידיאולוגיה של בחירת ציון, והיתה היסוד לתקוות ולאמונות משיחיות הכרוכות בבית דוד.

בהם עוסק עיון זה, דהיינו בסיפור העלאת הארון, בסיפור נבואת נתן ובסיפור המפקד והמגיפה, אנו מוצאים רמזים לביקורת עוקצנית או ביקורת גלוייה ותקיפה כנגד בית שאול. בסיפור המפקד והמגיפה (שמ"ב כד) אין הדברים גלויים. הם עולים רק מתוך האנאלוגיה. המפנה המשמעותי בסיפור זה חל לאחר דברי המחאה של דוד "הנה אנכי חטאתי ואנכי העויתי ואלה הצאן מה עשו" (שמ"ב כד 17), אך בסיפור על הרעב שנגרם בשל חטא בית שאול (שמ"ב כא), ואשר ישנם החושבים כי הוא קשור לסיפור המגיפה שבפרק כד, אין דוד משמיע דברי מחאה כאשר העם כולו נענש על חטאו של יחיד.

המסקנה יכולה אפוא להרמז, אך אינה מפורשת. ואילו בסיפור על נבואת נתן מוצהר במפורש, במרכזה של ההבטחה העיקרית לעתיד זרעו של דוד: "וחסדי לא יסור ממנו כאשר הסרתי מעם שאול אשר הסרתי מלפניך" (שמ"ב ז 15). הדברים ברורים עוד יותר בסיפור העלאת הארון. סיפור זה (שמ"ב ו) מרוכז סביב שתי אפיזודות: המעשה בעוזא והמעשה במיכל. ניתוח מבנה הפרק מראה שבמצבו הנוכחי שקולות שתי האפיזודות זו כנגד זו. ממילא, יוצא שלתוכנן חשיבות זהה ואין האחת משנית לרעותה. מבחינת המסר יוצא אם כן שבאותה מידה שחשוב היה לעורך־המחבר לספר שדוד הוא שעצר את זעמו של האל ולרמוז שדוד מביא לעירו אל שאינו מתפרץ עוד בזעם משחית וגחמני – היה חשוב לו גם לומר שבית שאול לא ידע להעריך מפעל זה ואת הברכה שבאה עמו, וחסדו של האל הוסר ממנו. כיוון שכך, מסתבר שהצגת מפעלו של דוד כהנחת יסודות לאמונה חדשה, דהיינו לתפיסה חדשה של האל, כרוכה במאבק כנגד בית שאול, או כנגד מי שמיוצג על ידי בית שאול. ישנם הסבורים כי הדברים על הסרת החסד מבית שאול מכוונים כנגד הממלכה הצפונית, ונאמרו סמוך לגלות שומרון. לדעתי אפשר שהדברים מוקדמים יותר, והם משקפים את ראיית מפעל דוד בפרספקטיבה של מפעל שלמה, דהיינו, הם שייכים לסיטואציה של עצם המאבקים סביב פילוג הממלכה.

אך העורך־המחבר אינו מסתפק בהצגת דוד כמניח יסודות לאמונה חדשה. הוא מציגו גם כמי שאירגן את ממלכתו בהתאם לעקרונותיה של אמונה זו. לשם כך אסף העורך־המחבר חומר רשימתי וערכו לשרותה של מטרה זו. שמ"ב ה הינו אוסף של ידיעות. הן מובאות בקצרה ובמקוטע; הן מהוות מדגם של פעילות דוד בכל התחומים. היסוד הבולט המהווה חוט־מקשר ומרכיב־מצרף בכל הידיעות הללו הוא נוכחותו של ה' בכל המפעלים והכרתו של דוד בנוכחות זו. המסר החד־משמעי ברשימה סיכומית זו הוא אפוא שדוד, בכל מעשיו ובכל מפעליו, הכיר שה' היה עמו והביאו לכל השגיו. ארגון הממלכה כרוך אפוא באידיאולוגיה מוגדרת. מסקנות זהות עולות גם מהעיון בחומר רשימתי אחר

ההנחות בדבר השינויים בדת שחולל דוד, או לפחות, שנתחוללו בממלכת יהודה, עשויות להתחזק במידה ניכרת על ידי השוואות אל המציאות שבממלכה הצפונית, כפי שהיא משתקפת במיוחד מספר מלכים. עיון בספר מלכים, ובמיוחד בספורי הנביאים, יחשוף לעיני הקורא מציאות דתית בממלכה הצפונית, שהיא שונה ביסודה מזו של הממלכה הדרומית. בשל אופן הצגת איש האלהים ודרכי פעולתו, נראה שאפשר ללמוד גם איך נתפס האל שבשמו פועל איש האלהים. איש האלהים מייצג את הצדק ואת המוסר, והוא פועל לעזרת העניים והסובלים. אך אופן פעולתו קרוב ביסודו לזה של איש המאגיה או המאנטיקן. על פי הופעתו הראשונה של אליהו אפשר ללמוד כי תפקידו הגלוי והמובן מאליו היה של מוריד גשמים, ונראה שאף המחבר־העורך הכיר בזאת, שכן, הוא מציגו לראשונה אגב ההצהרה "חי ה' אלהי ישראל אשר עמדתי לפניו אם יהיה השנים האלה טל ומטר כי אם לפי דברי" (מל"א יז 1). אך המאפיינים החוזרים ונשנים בסיפורי הנביאים קושרים את איש האלהים בריפוי חולים; בדיבורו מצוי לרוב יסוד חידתי ובפעולתו יש לעתים קרובות יסוד כמעט מאגי, אם לא מאגי ממש. תופעה זו בולטת יותר בסיפורי אלישע מאשר בסיפורי אליהו: בדברי אליהו בולטת תמיד ההדגשה שהוא פועל בשם ה' ושה' הוא המחולל את המעשים, בעוד שאלישע פועל לעתים בלי לפנות כלל אל ה'. כמו כן, מובלטת בסיפורי אליהו וגם בסיפורי אלישע הסכנה שבמגע עם איש האלהים ובפגיעה בו: הסיפור על אליהו ושלשת שרי החמשים (מל"ב א) והסיפור על אלישע והנערים שהדובים הרגום (מל"ב ב 23–25) מלמדים שאפילו פגיעה קלה בכבודו של איש האלהים כרוכה בסכנת מוות.

על פי מאפיינים אלה ניתן לשער שאיש האלהים מייצג אל שיש בו הרבה מן המסתורי והבלתי מובן, אשר ניתן להטות את רצונו גם על ידי פעולות מאגיות, ואשר תגובותיו אלימות ומתפרצות, גם ללא אזהרה. מאפיינים אלה אינם מצויים בתאורי פעולתו של איש האלהים ביהודה, ובהופעותיו נמצא שהוא מייצג אל הפועל על פי אמות מידה מוסריות, גלויות וברורות. יוצא אפוא שעריכתם הסופית של ספרי נביאים ראשונים מכירה בקיומן של שתי מציאויות דתיות שונות: זו שבצפון וזו שבדרום, ואם אין העורך של ספר מלכים גם עורכו של ספר שמואל (ובמיוחד שמ"ב), ממילא יוצא שאכן קיימת בממלכה הצפונית מציאות דתית שונה מזו שבדרומית. ניתן להניח אפוא שאותם שינויים אשר מבקש, לדעתי, מחברו של ספר שמ"ב לייחס לדוד – לא נקלטו בממלכה הצפונית, ושם כמסתבר, המשיכו להתקיים מסורות שמקורותיהם שונים.

עיון מפורט במבנה הסיפורים עשוי לשקף גם את הסיטואציה ההיסטורית אשר הולידה את הצורך במסריהם הייחודיים. בשלושת הסיפורים המרכזיים

את הברכה הצפויה בעקבות מפעליו של דוד. זהו, ככל הנראה, הרעיון המרכזי המונח ביסוד הקונפליקט שבסיפור העלאת הארון ובסיפור המגיפה. קביעתם של שני סיפורים אלה במקומם הנוכחי, דהיינו – העלאת הארון כמעשה הראשון שעשה דוד לאחר מולכו על כל ישראל ולאחר כיבוש ירושלים, וקניית גורן ארונה – כמעשה המשמעותי האחרון, יצרו, כאמור, מסגרת ספרותית שבעזרתה מבקש המחבר־העורך להדגיש את משמעותו של מפעל דוד כמהפכה בתחום האמונה והדת.

דברים אלה מתחדדים עם העיון בסיפור על נבואת נתן שבשמ"ב ז. על רצונו של דוד לבנות בית לה', משיב ה', בפי נתן, בשלילה. נתוח הכתוב תוך התייחסות להקשרו ולמקומות האחרים במקרא בהם נזכר הדבר (מל"א ה 17; דה"א כב 8, דה"א יז 4), יגלה שהתנגדותו של ה' אינה התנגדות למי שיקים את הבית אלא לעצם הקמת הבית. בשאלה "האתה תבנה לי בית לשבתי" (שמ"ב ז 5) יש לשים את הדגש על המילה "לשבתי" ולא על המילה "האתה". הנימוק הצמוד לכך מחזק טענה זו, שכן, האל מצהיר כי לא ישב בבית מיום העלותו את בני ישראל ממצרים, אלא התהלך באהל ובמשכן. בהקשר זה אין ספק שיציאת מצרים נתפסת כמאורע מכונן, שעל כן פירושה של ההכרזה מרחיק אותנו אל מעבר להזכרת עובדה היסטורית בפי האל: האל אינו מזכיר את יציאת מצרים אלא כדי להבהיר שמאז היותו לעם הזה לאל הנו אל המתהלך באהל ובמשכן. הרצון להושיבו בבית מנוגד אפוא לעצם מהותו. בפרק כולו מתגלות שתי מערכות של ביטויים ומושגים: האחת היא של ביטויי ארעי, נדודים והתהלכות; והשנייה היא של ביטויי קבע, יציבות ונצחיות. דברים אלה מסייעים לביסוס ההנחה שהקונפליקט האמיתי שבסיפור זה הוא סביב שתי תפיסות של האל, והמאבק הוא בין ישן לבין חדש. ההבטחות המפורשות המושמעות בפי נתן בשם האל מבהירות מהו פתרונו של האל בקונפליקט זה: העתיד כולו מושתת על תפיסת הקבע: זרעו של דוד, אשר ישב על כסאו, הוא שיבנה בית לה'; אך בית זה, על פי ההקשר, מתגלה בעיקרו כערובה למערכת יחסים מיוחדת וחדשה בין האל ובין בית דוד: חסדו של האל לא יסור ממנו, וענשי האל על חטאים לא יהיו עוד כפי שנהג להעניש בעבר. האל נותן אפוא את ברכתו לדרכו של דוד. בית ה', שבוודאי עומד על תילו בשעה שדברים אלה מסופרים, משמש בעיני המחבר הוכחה לצדקת דרכו של דוד, ואפשר לומר שלצרכיו הרטוריים של המחבר, חשובה קדושת הבית פחות מאשר ההוכחה לנצחיות בית דוד ולצדקת מפעליו. עם זאת, ככלות הכל – הבית לא נבנה בימי דוד, שעל כן מתברר מה רבה היתה באמת מידת המתח והחרדה שליוו את מפעליו. דוד, כמסתבר, נאלץ לוותר, וכך מתגלה תמונת המציאות שגרמה להיווצרותו של סיפור זה.

תמצית

שני סיפורים מהווים מעין מסגרת סיפורית למפעליו של דוד לאחר שמלך על כל ישראל. הסיפור האחד הוא מעשה העלאת הארון לירושלים (שמ״ב ו), והסיפור השני הוא המעשה במפקד ובמגיפה שנגרמה בגללו (שמ״ב כד).

משמעותה של מסגרת זו מתבהרת משעומדים על היסודות המשותפים שבשני הסיפורים. בשניהם יוזם דוד מבצע ראוותני ובשניהם מעורר הדבר, מסיבה שאינה מחוורת דיה, את זעמו של האל, המפעיל את כוחו הממית. בשני הסיפורים מגלה עיון נוסף כי למבצעו של דוד יש משמעות מעבר לתחום הגלוי והחיצוני: העלאת הארון אינה רק אקט דתי־סמלי כי אם גם פעולה בעלת תוצאות ארגוניות־פוליטיות. המפקד, לעומת זאת, אינו רק אקט ארגוני, כי אם מעשה שיש לו גם השלכות דתיות. בשני הסיפורים מצליח דוד להפוך את זעמו של האל לברכה, לאחר הבעת מחאה: בסיפור העלאת הארון מחאתו של דוד מתבטאת בסרובו להמשיך ולהעלות את הארון, ובסיפור המגיפה מוחה דוד באמרו: ״הנה אנכי חטאתי ואנכי העויתי ואלה הצאן מה עשו...״ (שמ״ב כד 17).

עיון מפורט יותר מעלה את האפשרות שהמחבר־העורך האחראי למבנהו של ספר שמואל ב׳ רואה במפעלו של דוד מפנה קיצוני בתחום הדת. מפנה זה מתבטא באופן תפיסתו של האל וממילא בדרכי האמונה בו, והוא כרוך בקביעת דפוסים ומסגרות חדשים בחיי הדת. העלאת הארון לירושלים וקניית גורן ארונה כדי להקים שם את הבית לה׳ אינם אלא שני צדדים של פעולה אחת. הרצון לעבוד אל המצוי בקביעות במקום אחד, עומד בניגוד לתפיסת האל כאל נודד או ׳מתהלך׳. אל נודד הוא גם אל שמנהגיו אינם צפויים מראש. הוא מתגלה או מסתתר כרצונו ואין לדעת מתי ייענה לדורשיו, אם ייענה. אל זה אף נתון להתפרצויות זעם שסיבותיהן, לעתים, אינן מחוורות כלל. אל היושב בבית, לעומת זאת, הוא אל הנענה לדורשיו בכל עת, ולהתנהגותו אמות מידה ברורות ומוסברות והן מושתתות על ערכים מוגדרים. האל הנודד וה׳מתהלך׳ מזוהה עם המשטר השבטי ועם מסורת השבטים, בעוד שהאל היושב בביתו ממצה בתכונותיו את הסמלים והאידיאלים ההולמים משטר ממלכתי. סביר אפוא להניח שהתנגדות למפעליו של דוד מקורה במי שדבק במסורות הקודמות. אפשר להניח שהחרדה מפני השינויים, היא זו המתגלה בדמות של זעם אלהי משחית. במלים אחרות, תאורי הזעם האלהי הנורא הם בעיקרם אזהרה מצד מי שמאמין בתום לבו כי השינויים שעומד דוד לחולל הם הרי אסון. המחבר מתמודד עם בעייה זו בהפכו את זעם האל לברכה, ובכך הוא מבטיח למתנגדים

סיכום 137

קיצורים קיצורים ביבליוגרפיים 141
קיצורים אחרים 181

מפתחות מפתח מראי מקום במקרא 185
מפתח מחברים 191

תמצית עברית 200

תוכן העניינים

פתיחה

מבוא 9
איש האלהים 15
הקשר להיסטוריה 20
אל זועם 25
תכניתו של דוד והתכנית האלהית 28

פרק ראשון: **העלאת הארון לירושלים (שמ"ב ו)** 33
המעשה בעוזא 36
האם חטא דוד? 42
היחס בין המעשה בעוזא והמעשה במיכל 46

פרק שני: **המפקד ועצירת המגיפה (שמ"ב כד)** 55
השוואה אל דה"א כא 59

פרק שלישי: **שמ"ב פרק ו ופרק כד** 69

פרק רביעי: **שמ"ב ז: אל 'יושב בית' או אל 'מתהלך באהל ובמשכן'?** 75
גישות לסיפור 75
מבנה וחיבור 80
משמעות הסיפור 89
עתיד ועבר 92
נבואת נתן ותפילת דוד 101
שמ"ב ז 26 102
טבלת המבנה 105

פרק חמישי: **שמ"ב ה: מבנה ומשמעות** 111
מאפיינים כלליים 114
ניתוח מפורט 115
המכנה המשותף 132

ספרים קודמים בסדרת עיונים במקרא ובתקופתו:

א: א. רופא, ספר בלעם.
ב: טליה רודין־אוברסקי, מאלוני ממרא עד סדום.
ג: ע. טוב, תרגום השבעים ככלי עזר במחקר המקרא. [אנגלית]
ד: נ. נאמן, גבולות ונחלות בהיסטוריוגרפיה המקראית: הרשימות הגיאוגרפיות במקרא. [אנגלית]

ISBN 965-242-007-7

נדפס במפעלי דפוס בן־צבי, ירושלים

עיונים במקרא ובתקופתו

ה

דוד ואלהיו
השתקפות אמונות ודעות בהיסטוריוגרפיה ובספור המקראי

שמאי גלנדר

סימור בע"מ

ירושלים תשנ"א